Behold the Man

People, Politics, and Events
Surrounding the Life of Jesus

George Cornell

A Key-Word book

WORD BOOKS, PUBLISHER
WACO, TEXAS

BEHOLD THE MAN

A KEY-WORD BOOK
Published by Pillar Books for Word Books, Publishers

First Key-Word edition published December 1976

ISBN: 0-87680-823-2

Library of Congress Catalog Card Number: 74-78044

Copyright © 1974 by Word, Incorporated

Printed in the United States of America

WHAT OTHERS SAY:

"Cornell has done the research and presents his readers with the facts in a dynamic style that compels us to behold the man Jesus in the light of his own time in history."

—Colorado Springs Sun

"(Cornell) is a challenging and imaginative writer and his subjects come alive in his fluent prose. . . .
"It is a book almost without beginning or end. Pick it up and turn to any page, and you are soon engrossed with its language, its style, its wonderment and its hope."

—Springfield Leader and Press

"Covering the life of Jesus in the manner of a modern newspaper reporter, George Cornell . . . has woven a tapestry of reality that makes the reader experience the sights, sounds, and events of Bible times. . . ."

—Hyannis Standard-Times

". . . An absorbing retelling of the story of Jesus by a journalist who has respect for both sources and style. . . ."

—The Review of Books and Religion

"Oursler called Him 'The Man Nobody Knows,' but after reading Cornell, one knows Him a little better."

—Pasadena Evening Star News

For a good man,
my son Harrison

Contents

Preface

The personalities, events, and conditions that formed the background for the drama of Jesus are presented here in narrative style, but they adhere firmly to the factual record. They are historical tales, drawn from the Bible, additional early Christian writings, and ancient secular history, with conjectural detail added only to describe moods, atmosphere, and other incidentals appropriate to the recorded facts. Nothing has been added, however, to distort or detract from that factual framework. It is only fleshed out and given its human components consistent with the evidence.

In connection with the Magi, all sorts of traditions about them were perpetuated in early Christian times by the church fathers—a process that continued into the Middle Ages, yielding a harvest of legends, imaginative stories, and perhaps some facts. Material in these varied accounts has been weighed against the historical and Gospel data, with whatever survives the test retained in substance but without the conflicting details. Rationalists dismiss the Magi story as sheer myth, but except for the supernatural attributes given the star, the story squares with the conditions, viewpoints, and pursuits existing at the time in the ancient east. Subsequent calculations by sixteenth century astronomer Johannes Kepler and ancient Chinese star records offer evidence that there was some phenomenal celestial activity in that era.

Information about King Herod and Pontius Pilate comes chiefly from the lengthy histories of Flavius Josephus, a Jewish scholar who became a supporter of imperial Rome, and whose volumes, *The Jewish Antiquities, Wars of the Jews* and *Josephus Against Apion,* provide the most detailed secular accounts of that period in Judea. Supplementary details about Herod and Pilate are taken from other extrabiblical sources such as the Gospel of Nicodemus. These also are used, along with the Bible, in portraying the general conditions prevailing at the time.

In some cases, particularly in the section on the prophets and Pentecost, direct quotations of individuals have been taken from their books or letters. Some dialogue has been drawn from noncanonical material and from Josephus, especially in regard to Herod and Pilate, and in a few minor instances is surmised.

The Scripture used throughout is based upon the Revised Standard Version, although paraphrased at times to keep the narrative flow alive.

For the most part, these accounts were written originally for the Associated Press and published by member newspapers in Christmas and Easter seasons of recent years. My thanks to Associated Press for allowing reproduction of those serials, which have been revised to some extent for publication in this form.

Although the story, for the most part, is arranged chronologically, some of it overlaps to a degree in time since each focuses on a different aspect of the story or on particular individuals involved in it. This is the case in regard to the section on the prophets which follows chapters concerning Jesus' nativity but which, of course, occurred beforehand. Largely, however, the sections relate in sequence the unfolding of a life that continually summons us to its completeness.

GEORGE W. CORNELL

PART 1
Seekers and the Sword

1.
Journey to Jesus

As he had done each evening for months, Melchior climbed the circular stairs of the tower atop Mount Vaus. He reached the roof, breathing heavily. He spread his maps on the stand and rested his arms there, gazing into the eastern quarter of the heavens. His colleagues would be here shortly. The time cycle already had entered its penultimate phase, and they awaited a sign of its completion—the supreme "fravashi" foretold of old.

It was a spring dusk in the 31st year of the reign of the Parthian King Phraates IV in Persia (6 B.C.). For the company of Rab-Mag Melchior, nature and careful computations had combined to bring about a state of acute vigilance. They were Magi, the most renowned scholars of the age, members of the imperial order of priests, royal counselors and masters of ancient, recondite sciences that would be lost to the centuries to come.

"Guide us aright, thou living god, Ahura Mazda." Melchior lifted his bearded face as the first glints flecked the sky. "Oh, thou creator of life, primeval spirit, thou wise one, give light to us who seek thy truth."

For nearly a year, as modern astronomy has since confirmed, a startling sequence of celestial phenomena had unfolded before these mystic sages. By their logic, the occurrences were more than enough to arouse keen suspense. But in addition, there are specific biblical and historical intimations that they had even weightier information to alert them at the time Jesus was born.

The evidence must have obsessed the elderly Melchior (one of varying names ascribed to him by early church tradition) as he and the other Magian noblemen gathered that night on their high lookout above the clear uplands of Persia. They wore long, white robes, tied at the waist with silken sashes. Embroidered figures of a crescent moon and the planets adorned the rims of their caps. As darkness deepened, they spoke quietly but intently of the implications they confronted.

These were no ordinary astrologers, soothsayers, or magicians of the kind that later misused the title, *magi*. Rather, they were profound theorists with concepts transcending their times and which still are in the forefront of abstract physics today.

"An auspicious night," Melchior commented, as he ambled about the platform, making sure each observer was at his assigned sector and had measuring dividers and bar. "Would that we could measure as well, my brothers, the visions of the inner eye."

To these authorities of the remote, mysterious Zend-Avesta, knowledge came not from facts alone, but by finding in them the expression of spiritual laws—by piercing the tangible to learn the truth it signified.

They perceived a grand, divine interlinking of all time and space, from the least particle to the cosmos. Each material appearance was relative, a mere manifestation of a basic substance all harmonized by a common, universal force. To decipher its majestic messages, they studied the earth, water, the air—and the fiery stars.

Melchior, back at his desk, gave his associates a final

reminder. "Take heed, my brothers. The finger of life oft writes in smallest script." Above, the Pleiades winked and Aldebaran blazed red on the forehead of the bull.

"Tomorrow, a month hence, who can know? We have applied our subtlest mathematics, and looked long into the face of the fire. But who is man to read the hour of the Omnipotent? And yet, perchance, tonight!" By every indication, they had available the cryptic, messianic time—data set down by the astounding Jewish seer, Daniel, who five centuries before held powerful sway in the courts of Persian kings.

The Magi, as the land's ancestral savants, had opportunity then to grasp the enigmatic chronology for the coming of the Great One as given by the honored foreigner, Daniel, in his seventh, eighth, and twelfth books. They also could preserve his prophecies of the event: "Behold, one like the Son of man came with the clouds of heaven . . . and there was given to him glory and everlasting dominion which shall not pass away."

Beyond this, however, other tenuous factors linked the Magi with Israel's hope of a redeemer. Abraham dwelt in Ur of the Chaldees, which modern archaeology has located on the Persian Gulf. Origins of the Magi's religion, of which Zoroaster was only a latter-day reformer, go deep into that same antiquity. Perhaps Melchizedek, priest of the Most High God to whom Abraham paid tribute, was one of them. Only they and the Jews, in all the pagan world, believed in one supreme deity.

The Magi's faith, too, foresaw a deliverer, Sosiosh, who would bestow everlasting, incorruptible life to mankind. Their archives also may well have included many of the Jewish prophecies of a savior. Moreover, centuries before, the famed diviner Balaam, son of Boer, a gentile like the Magi and also from the "mountains of the east," delivered his stunning oracle as recounted in Numbers.

"There shall come a star out of Jacob, and a Scepter shall rise out of Israel. . . . He that shall have dominion."

So the Magi, endowed with their abstruse time deductions and the intermingled prescience of the past, had reason to watch the heavens. To them each turn of earthly destiny was reflected in nature, a "fravashi," and they sought to detect it.

Three times in the past ten months marvelous displays (as determined by the astronomer Kepler 1,600 years later), had paraded before their gaze. On the fourteenth day of last Simanu (our May 29), the planets Saturn and Jupiter conjoined in the 21st degree of the constellation Pisces, close to the first point of Aries, the ram—a zone deemed fraught with significance. Just four months later, on the twelfth of Tashritum (September 27), another conjunction of the same planets occurred in the 16th degree of Pisces, and two months later, on the twenty-fifth of Tabitum (December 5), retrograde motion brought the two spheres together again.

It had now been four months since the last spectacle. To the Magi, four was a perfect number, represented in the four basic elements. If a fourth conjunction occurred, they could only conclude some prodigious meaning. Melchior's old eyes roved with practiced familiarity among the sidereal landmarks. As Pisces wheeled above the eastern horizon, he trained his attention there. Tidings in the constellation of fishes had the noblest import.

Shortly, his arm rose and he pointed a shaking finger. "Lo! The heavens speak!" There, against the jeweled blackness, not only the great planets Jupiter and Saturn converged, but Mars, too, joining in a resplendent trigon.

Awed exclamations burst out on the rooftop and some Magians dropped to their knees. Gradually, however, they grew silent, watching the luminous solar embrace. Stillness, deep as the reaches of space, settled over them. But then, suddenly, as if a door of a pit had opened to the sun, a new light flashed in the eastern firmament. A new star, a stella nova, a flame no astronomer ever proved or postulated, burst into the world's night.

Its brightness washed the earth. Its rays glittered like points of a crown. It opened its sublime might to the tired and groping, and silver dusted the city below and trimmed the ridges of the mountains of Zagros.

The Magi saw their star in the east. There in a land where the mystic wisdom of the Orient mingled with a faith older than history. There in the land of the nightingale and the rose, above the high plateau of Persia, a star appeared.

No one knows its nature. Ne record remains of it in the astral lore of Babylon. Whatever man's instruments or research may disclose has no bearing on that star. For the Magi saw it—with their eyes and in their hearts.

"Arise . . . for thy light is come, and the glory of the Lord is risen upon thee. . . ." So Isaiah had written. "And the gentiles shall come to thy light. They shall bring gold and incense; and they shall show forth the praises of the Lord."

It had taken nearly three months to prepare for the 1,500-mile journey. Shouts of leather-shirted cavalry officers mingled with the bawl of animals as supplies were loaded. The chief cameleer rushed about, yelling instructions and gesturing violently, as sweating slaves hoisted rope crates and grain bags to the backs of kneeling freight beasts. Dust swirled in the bright Persian sunlight.

Blankets, tents, foodstuffs, water casks, and other necessities, along with chests of rare treasures, were stowed on the wooden pack saddles, divided equally by weight on either side, and bound to the uprights.

Since it would be a rigorous trip, only about 400 pounds of cargo, two-thirds the usual maximum, was placed on each camel. A crowd of jostling townspeople looked on, women veiled in their chadors; dark, hirsute men with laughing eyes. "A fool's expedition!" they said. "Those gray beards chase the wind."

Behind a brick wall, inside the palace of the royal Magian Council, a circle of white-gowned men sat around a fire, staring silently into its leaping flames. Among them were the three (the number and their identifications are matters of divergent ancient accounts, but the most common listing is used here) who had determined to track the genesis of a star.

They were Melchior, pale, old, white-bearded; Gaspar, a tall, ruddy young priest; and blackskinned Balthazar, of medium age and stature, whose ancestors may have come to Persia in the days when its empire stretched to Ethiopia.

Not all their fellow Magi condoned this quest to honor a hypothetical "Blessed One" of alien birth. Nor would they, as the ensuing years proved, accept its validity. It smacked of national disloyalty. But the tenacity of High Magus Melchior and his supporters had overcome this narrow view. The strange mission was decreed.

Seeking divine guidance, the counselors sat now to contemplate the beams of the fire with a most pious mind. So their prophet, Zarathustra, had taught. So Moses heard God on fiery Sinai and in a burning bush.

Presently, Melchior stirred from his reverie. He picked up a worn, yellowed scroll, passed it through the curling smoke of a censer and read slowly. "And the Lord will lift up an ensign to the nations from afar. . . . And his name shall be called Wonderful . . . the Mighty God . . . the Prince of Peace."

There were murmurs, both of dissent, and approval, for this was an old Jewish oracle. But then Melchior read from their own age-old writings in the Avestan, which said: "In that time, the Ruler in Truth shall arise. He shall slay death . . . and perpetuate the dead. He shall make all things new."

No man spoke.

Finally, the group rose and filed out of the altar room. After farewell embraces, the three travelers donned their turbans and fur-trimmed cloaks, strode out to the waiting train and mounted their dromedaries.

"Khikh!" The guttural command burst from the cameleers. They jerked at the halters, and the beasts rose, growling, to their feet. The troop of mounted bowmen moved forward, the golden eagle of Persia fluttering on their banners. The long trek was on. The caravan climbed the steep trails into the mountains on Persia's western rim, and descended into the lowlands beyond. Wild boars, cheetahs, and other carnivores infested the area, while bulbuls sang from the box trees.

In what city the march began is uncertain, but since the Magian priesthood served as one of the two councils to the king, it may have been at Hecatompylos, the northern capital "of a hundred gates." Or, they may have left from the winter castle in Ctesiphon, with its stately domes and arcades, or from the former hundred-columned capital at Persepolis, or the once-sovereign western city, Susa.

Here was said to be the tomb of the Jewish prophet Daniel, who had served as a Persian viceroy. Ancient reports also suggest other points of origin. Explorer Marco Polo, in the Middle Ages wrote: "In Persia is the city called Saba from which the three wise men set out when they came to worship Jesus Christ."

At any rate, despite some traditions saying each of them came from different places such as Media, India, Tharsis, Arabia, Nibia, and Ethiopia, this is flatly refuted by the apostle Matthew who cites a single homeland—"their own country."

The overriding evidence is that this was Persia. In the original Greek, Matthew's Gospel specifies the

"Magi," who at the time of Jesus' birth and for centuries before, were widely known as the learned priestly caste of Persia. Matthew's original language also connotes "the Far East," and comparisons with other documents of the era show this was the common phrase used for the area of Persia.

The weight of tradition agrees. It may be that other nationalities sometimes mentioned refer to racial backgrounds, since in the past heyday of Persian empire, their regions had been included. Some still were.

Thus, the venturesome Magi, leaving behind Persia's barren expanse of Drangiana with its salt-water lakes and yapping jackals, traveled on through the wooded foothills of the Zagros.

The military escort was supplied as a routine to such royal entourages, even though the fratricidal King Phraates IV, dominated by an Italian concubine he called "the goddess Musa," had no taste for the mission.

The squadron of helmeted archers, with their fine-limbed horses, led the column down into the plain of Appolloniatis on past the proudly independent city of Seleucia beside the Tigris, and as far as the Euphrates bridge. For the troop of archers to go farther might have appeared warlike. The Magi and their retinue of servants likely continued from there alone. A long, hard road, of many months, lay ahead.

What kind of men were these who discerned a still small voice, and pursued it across a continent? The annals of that time tell of their knowledge and insight.

Philo, then an Alexandrian philosopher, said the Magi "behold the books of nature with more acute perception that usual." A contemporary Roman scholar, Apuleius, calls them "divinely wise."

The Wisdom of Solomon says the Magi "Seek for God being conversant with his works." The ancient Greek geographer, Herodotus, said that in all the world's ignorance was one shining exception—the truth-loving Magi.

Many other ancient scholars, Plutarch, Diogenes, Laertius, Pliny, all speak of the Magian acuity. Out of that insight—out of their intuitions and convictions about a star—they had drawn a faith that took them hundreds of miles, in broiling heat of day and chill of night, across the wide Syrian desert to Haleb or Tudmore, and on along the dusty highway to Damascus.

They tramped on. The saddles chaffed their legs; the sun burned their skin and dust caked their eyes. They camped at night in their black goathair tents, for it would not be fitting for regal personages to stop in foreign hostels with their dancers, boxers, knifethrowers, and comedians balancing underfed infants atop poles.

The brilliant star they had seen "in the east," or more specifically translated "at the rising," apparently did not guide them for Judea lay to the west beside the Mediterranean—not to the east.

The question spread through the city. It whipped along the shops of the marketplace. It filtered into the crowded quarter of the poor, the Acra, and swirled through the Temple courts. The question jarred Jerusalem:

"Where is he that is born king of the Jews?"

Old men frowned and young men wagged their heads. Clothmongers paused in their prattle and women clapped hands to their mouths. Some men scoffed; some shrugged; others dreamed. Some chewed their lips, wondering.

In the middle hour of the morning, the three strangers, potentates from a distant land, had ridden into the city and halted at the "broad place" just inside the fountain gate, asking their disturbing question: "Where is he that is born king . . . ? For we have seen his star in the east, and are come to worship him."

To the three windburned travelers, the learned Magi

of Persia, it must have been keenly dispiriting to find that here in the holy city, the very cradle of prophetic light, none knew of its culmination.

At last they reached the gates of Jerusalem. They proceeded on up the narrow streets, their footmen bearing gift cases. A growing throng of onlookers trailed behind them and on either side. Lictors, with bronze-tipped staves, cleared the way. The venerable, old Melchior swayed tiredly in the saddle, and voices babbled around them.

"What manner of excellencies are these? . . . They speak boldly of a new king. . . . Will not Herod seize them? . . . Are they mad? . . . Surely they are Asian princes. . . . They wear the emblems of wizards of the Far East. . . ."

All Jerusalem was troubled, Matthew's Gospel reports, for the question revived an age-old cry echoing out of the mists of the past in this enchanted city.

On the evening before, the impressive visitors had pitched camp in the Kidron Valley outside the walls. Their dark tents with fringed awnings drew swarms of beggars and waifs, whom the Magians ordered fed and given coins.

Now, after a restful night, they had entered the city, convinced they had reached the end of their long pilgrimage—the birthplace of the God-king. For this was the capital of the people predestined to be his lineage.

Yet the only response had been guarded looks, surprise, and perplexity. Roman sergeants appeared brusquely to ask the delegation its purpose, and other functionaries scrutinized them with questioning looks.

Beside a pool, Melchior raised his hand and the party halted. An attendant hurried up and the old High Magus eased himself to the ground, road sore and stiff. Balthazar and young Gaspar also dismounted. The three left their camels with servants and trudged silently up the paved ramp toward the Temple. It dominated the city, high on the eastern hill, its marble walls and towers gleaming in the sun.

Melchior squinted, his face drawn and dark. His own ancient religion, with its one great God of goodness, reared no earthly temples. Yet the bygone pontiff Persian kings had proclaimed Israel's God the same. He plodded along slowly, blinking at the shimmering stones ahead.

Long ago, the powerful Darius had decreed that the "God of Daniel" is the "living God," synonymous with Ahura-Mazda. And Cyrus the Great said likewise, even providing means to restore the Jewish Temple in all its grandeur.

Why, then, was the Divine Epiphany unknown here? Melchior ran a wrinkled hand over his face. Had he misread the accumulated perception of the age? Had he mistranslated a star?

How painstakingly his royal priestly academy had pored over obscure formulas, examined the elements and analyzed the time intervals given by Daniel to comprehend the supernal moment.

And then the planetary heralds had come, followed by the mystic flame—the "star of Jacob" as foreseen in a trance by the gentile deviner, Balaam. Yet, here where it had beckoned, its meaning remained unrealized. Had the search been in vain, a puerile illusion? Practical-minded men had called it so. Could they be right? Was the search for a savior sheer folly?

Melchior sighed and suddenly he was deeply weary, drained of all energy. He hesitated unsteadily there on the sloping pavement, and again pressed a hand to his eyes. Balthazar gripped his shoulder. "Art thou faint, Rab-Magus?"

Sometimes in the human makeup, when the mind is disciplined to its finest edge, when flesh is hammered so thin as to give outlet to the soul, the door also is open to assaults from without threatening the delicate poise of reason. A severe disappointment, the shattering of a life's conviction and purpose, could wreck the thin balance. It could, if a man let it.

Melchior set his jaw, waved Balthazar away and pushed on up the hill. He would not lose heart! Failure was impossible! God did not change. His covenant remained undiminished. Only man's understanding of it veered and wavered, for he judged truth in a moment's narrow scope, not the sweep of the eternity.

All that was, had been, or would be, existed always in God, including now. Had not then his Emissary come, his staff been raised on earth? Melchior clasped his hands at his chest as he walked on. On a portico outside the Temple wall, the Magi approached a rabbi who sat awaiting his students, and explained briefly the object of their search.

A light, an old hunger, darted in the teacher's eyes, and then he frowned, glancing about uneasily. "Thou dost stir up the wells of hope," he said in a low voice. "Withal, be heedful lest the Herodians take thy words amiss. The king is a jealous king."

Melchior smiled wanly, and his hand traced a circle, the sign of blessing. The search went on. They inquired of chief priests, in the shops, among the lowly and high.

Soon a bowing courtier came to their tents, garbed in ornamented robes and pendants, who addressed them unctuously: "Honored sirs, I bring thee greetings from his majesty, Herod the King, who requests audience with thee that he may attend thee in thy desires."

Melchior nodded thoughtfully.

A squad of Roman troops led them across the city to the west wall. As the gates swung open to the lavish castle, with its sweeping esplanade, fountains and arbors, trumpet blasts sounded from a tower.

Compared to the troubled buzzing of the city without, a troubled quiet descended within the palace grounds.

2.
The Fox

Dismissing his hairdresser, King Herod slipped on a light, elegant evening robe, quaffed deeply from a silver beaker of Greek Chian wine, his favorite, and sent a slave running to fetch his wife, Mariamne. The hours ahead would haunt him to his grave, but he did not know that now.

He slumped down on an ermine-covered ivory couch and waited, momentarily pleased with himself, exulting at how he had maneuvered Augustus Caesar into retaining him as king of this unruly Jewish realm, eager for Mariamne's embraces.

Then she stood there before him—beautiful, exquisite as always, but with pained defiance in her eyes. "I have come as you have commanded," she said, "but only to tell thee openly, I find thy companionship no longer supportable."

His face clouded and alternate waves of outrage, bewilderment, jealousy, impotence, and fury went through him. He loved her, the one person in all the merciless, tyrannical, trustless jungle of his life that he did love. Although he did not yet realize it, he would destroy the only person he loved, just as he would seek to destroy the very incarnation of utmost love itself.

Herod finished off the wine and stared down at his fawn-skin slippers, shaking his head. It was happening again—the designs against him, the undermining and conniving that already had drenched his house in blood. But the nearness of her, the scent of her perfume, the overwhelming feeling he had for her swept over him and he stood up, declaring his great effections and swearing his devotion.

"Yes," she said cuttingly, "thou didst to be sure demonstrate thy love to me by the injunctions thou gavest to Sohemus when thou commanded him to kill me if any harm came to thee from Caesar."

Herod flew into a rage. So she knew. She obviously had wormed it out of his aide, Sohemus, and she could have done that only through intimacies. He hurled the wine beaker across the room.

"Debauched!" he screamed at her. "Adulteress!"

She denied it vehemently and fled the room.

Indeed, on Herod's visit to Augustus, he had left Mariamne and her mother, Alexandra, under Sohemus' watch, with instructions to execute them in case he was slain for opposing Augustus in his war against Mark Antony. Herod's twisted purpose had been to forestall a re-ascendancy of Jewish royalty, of which his wife and mother-in-law were members. But his mission had turned out differently and he had won the backing of Augustus. Now, instead of it being celebrated, he met what he deemed treachery.

The ensuing events followed a pattern unvarying in Herod's regime—interrogations, lies, intrigue, torture, violence, and death. It had been that way ever since he seized the Judean throne by force, massacring resisters, wiping out the reigning Jewish line, including many of Mariamne's relatives.

She was a Jewish princess of the Hasmonean house. This was the dynasty that had ruled since the uprising of the heroic Maccabees against the Syrians in 166 B.C., restoring Judean independence. Years later, this dynasty had been ruthlessly crushed by Rome and Herod. Herod had ten wives, but his marriage to Mariamne had brought an authentic Jewish element into his court, although he himself preferred the pagan cultures of Greece and Rome.

He was obsessed with her as a woman, but resentful of her stubborn faith in one universal God. He scorned her just as he did Judaism itself and its people. Because they "preferred righteousness to glory, that nation was not agreeable to him," writes the historian Josephus. "He was conscious that he was hated by those under him."

Their Jewish faith, going far back to the origins of human civilization in the Tigris-Euphrates region, was much older than the polytheism of Greece and Rome, or the oriental religions of Buddhism, Hinduism, and later Islam. Yet it was only a tiny enclave generally ignored by the world at large.

Religiously, it was an amorphous atmosphere, a mixed brew of many gods, myths and superstitions. The gods of wind, sea and soil, of war and reproduction, of the Greek Zeus, Hera, Ares and Aphrodite, blended with the matching Roman deities of Jupiter, Juno, Mars, and Diana. Merging with this celestial roster were the innumerable gods from Egypt and the mystical east, gods of many hands, of many breasts, gods with heads of crocodiles, goats, and cats.

And Caesar Augustus smiled as choruses chanted, "Ave Caesar, Lord over all aeons, highest of the high."

"A beast . . . with ten horns and seven heads with ten diadems upon its horns and blasphemous name upon its head," said the apocalyptic first-century Book of Revelation in veiled condemnation of Rome's imperial rule. "The whole earth followed the beast . . .

and they worshipped the beast, saying, 'Who is like the beast, and who can fight it?' "

There were sacred groves, stones, animals, and brooks. Wonder-working thaumaturgists roved the countryside and processions of white-robed priests served in the lofty temples, reciting from the riddles of the Sibylline books. Augurs deciphered the wishes of the gods by flights of birds, thunder, the way oil spread on a saucer of water, or by examining the liver of a sheep. Hepatoscopy, it was called. Statues of Vesta, in wood or stone, stood on household altars, the *lares familiaris*. It was a time of syncretism, of a blurring, colliding congeries of idolatries, magic, divinations, spells, astrologers, oracles, portents, and bizarre secret rites.

"Do not tell thy secret, friend," initiates into the mysteries were warned.

Besides the official state pantheons headed by the corresponding Greek Zeus and Roman Jupiter, the empire churned with many other cults spread from Assyria, Egypt, and Asia Minor by the shuttling of Roman armies. In the widely extensive worship of the Asian fertility goddess, Cybele, participants whirled in frenzied dances, slashing their own flesh, then writhed in the gore beneath a sacrificed bull on a grated altar —the taurobolium.

There was also widespread devotion to the cow-headed Egyptian goddess, Isis, the favorite of Cleopatra. The mythical reanimation of her murdered lover, Osiris, was celebrated in elaborate rites using phallic symbols and a mulberry coffin. A first-century inscription to Serapis, another name for Osiris, still shows on the Zion gate in the south wall of old Jerusalem.

Augustus himself once was initiated into the popular Eleusian mysteries, centered on the Greek goddess Demeter, also known as Kore or Persephone. The orgiastic cycle of worship lasted three days at a time. Herod built a sanctuary to her in Samaria, another to the god Pan in Caesarea Philippi, a frequent scene of Jesus' ministry.

Some of the wildest rites focused on the Greek god of wine, Dionysus, the Roman Bacchus. To beating cymbals, drums, and flutes, devotees fondled serpents, let young animals suckle women, then tore them apart and ate them raw as they whipped themselves into a catalyptic trance of *entheoi*—indwelt by the god.

Commonfolk often joined many cults, not fully trusting any. Urbane skeptics doubted all of them. Greek stoics and Roman cynics said only sheer rationalism mattered. Epicureans stressed escape into pleasure.

But Augustus, often called a reincarnation of the god Mercury, strove to invigorate the official cults, rebuilding eighty-two temples, restaffing them with priests and vestal virgins, encouraging emperor worship as a test of patriotism in the provinces—a rising practice that eventually would mark Jews and the followers of Jesus as seditious atheists.

In the midst of this motley religious milieu, Judaism stood like a resisting citadel. Despite the pressures of infiltrating Greco-Roman ways, Judaism upheld its ancient faith in one, unifying Lord of history, revealed through centuries of events and recorded in the Scriptures.

"Hear O Israel, the Lord our God, the Lord is one," went its immemorial Shema. Herod's wife, Mariamne, attended regularly in prayers, the reading of the law and the prophets, defying Greco-Roman tastes. She had admired Herod as a daring, young general, even loved him, but her esteem had turned to bitterness as his overriding lust for power and endless suspicions had led him to kill her grandfather, her father, her uncle, and brother.

The last case had occurred after her mother, Alexandra, had persuaded Cleopatra to get Mark Antony to compel Herod to name Mariamne's youthful brother, Aristobulus, as high priest. Herod had done so, but because of Aristobulus' popularity Herod promptly had him drowned while bathing in the river Jericho.

Antony, at the instigation of Cleopatra who had always sought Herod's domain for herself, had summoned Herod for an accounting of the death but had let him off. Thereafter, Mariamne had become increasingly cold toward her husband.

"Meanness of birth," she said of his Idumean relatives, particularly disliking his vindictive sister, Salome. And Salome had constantly impugned Mariamne to Herod, suggesting infidelities, falsely claiming Mariamne had sent her picture to Mark Antony to seek his courtship.

Herod, chronically inflamed with jealousies and distrust, had put Mariamne's mother in confinement. Following one of his absences, when Salome intimated that her own husband, Joseph, had been familiar with Mariamne, Herod had him beheaded.

Herod was not Jewish himself, but an Idumean from Arabian areas to the south. In his younger years, he had been a fiercely proficient warrior. Other soldiers would stand amazed at his power with the javelin, his accuracy with an arrow, the precision of his swordsmanship. He had been a skilled horseman and hunter. On one day alone, he cut down forty beasts—bears, stags, and wild asses.

He had gained and held his throne by skillfully shifting his alliances from one Roman overlord to another as the reins of power changed hands. He had learned these methods from his crafty father, Antipater, who himself had switched allegiances from Pompey, the Roman conqueror of the east in 63 B.C. to the rival who overpowered him, Julius Caesar.

It was under Julius Caesar that Herod first was named governor of Galilee and Samaria, but he had to fight for it. With 2,000 armed footmen and 200

horsemen, he had roved the territory, wiping out resistance, wreaking carnage on rebellious Galilean villages. He had captured and executed the rebel Jewish
guerrillas led by Hezekias, and at one point, lowered
soldiers in chests to the mouths of mountain caves,
using grappling hooks and fire to bring out the hold-
outs into the open where they were slain — men,
women, and children.

After Julius Caesar was murdered on the Ides of
March, 44 B.C., Herod had thrown his lot with the
assassins, Brutus and Cassius, who named him governor of all Syria. He had swept through Samaria, his
forces augmented by two legions of 6,000 men each
and 1,000 horsemen supplied by the Romans. He then
fought his way into Jerusalem for the first time in 43
B.C., putting to rout the Jewish heir to the throne.
Antigonus, whose nationalist forces would plague
Herod for years.

His ties to Brutus and Cassius had become question-
able when a combination was formed against them by
Octavius, Caesar's grand-nephew and adopted son
(who eventually became the emperor titled the Revered
One), Augustus, and his general, Mark Antony. Herod
had turned to wooing Antony, plying him with gold, in
return for which Antony named him tetrarch of Judea,
giving him an imperial title more fitting to his power.

However, an uprising by the army of Antigonus, in
league with the Parthians, siezed Jerusalem, and Herod
fled to Rome, ingratiating himself both with Octavius
and Antony. They jointly appointed him king of
Judea in the year 40, an act confirmed by the Roman
senate after half its members, including the famed
orator Cicero, was slain by Octavius' troops in solidify-
ing his control.

Herod, exulting his new kingship, returned to Judea.
Gathering his troops, and with additional forces supplied by Antony, he attacked Jerusalem. The seige went
on for two years, pressed with catapults, battering

rams, and towers for bowmen. Altogether Herod had eleven legions — 66,000 foot soldiers and 6,000 cavalrymen.

The city put up a stubborn, furious defense, its citizens sometimes striking out in hand-to-hand combat to destroy the siege weapons. But the Romans rebuilt them and finally crashed into the city, ravaging it and unleashing a rampage of killing in the streets, houses, and crowds. By that conquest in 37 B.C., Herod's Roman appointment as king of Judea became reality.

Only six years later, however, the Roman partnership that had sponsored him broke up. Octavius turned against the carousing Mark Antony who was moonstruck with Cleopatra in Egypt. Herod, gambling on the outcome of the conflict, supported his close patron, Antony. However, the sluggish fleet of Antony and Cleopatra went down to total defeat at Actium in the year 31 before the swift, small warships of Octavius. The outcome drove Antony and Cleopatra to suicide and put Herod in dire jeopardy.

For once, he had backed the wrong Roman, and his fate was uncertain. He had gone by ship to confront Octavius, newly titled, Augustus Caesar. Herod had known he might face summary execution, and in case it happened, he had left orders for Mariamne's death, too. But his bold approach to Augustus had succeeded.

Bluntly detailing how he had supported Antony to the utmost in the war of the Romans, Herod had told Augustus: "I desire that thou wilt first consider how faithful a friend, and not whose friend, I have been. Thou wilt find by experience that I shall do and be the same to thyself."

The gambit had worked, and Augustus had even enlarged Herod's Judean kingdom, returning to him rich lands of palms and balsam that Anthony had given Cleopatra. Herod, in high spirits once the imperial festivities were over, had summoned Mariamne to his chambers, only to be coldly rejected by her.

It had shattered his triumphant return and the old mistrust and fears snaked again through Herod's palace.

After Mariamne had spurned his attentions and fled his wrath to her chambers, Salome again fomented his suspicions. She sent a slave to him with a potion, misinforming him that Mariamne had mixed it for him. Believing it poison, Herod had the slave tortured on the rack, then killed. In his rage, he also executed Sohemus, the guard he had assigned to watch over Mariamne.

Then, in that curious inversion by which all destroyers turn on those they love most, he killed his one love. Hating her, loving her, wild with jealousy despite her denials, his manhood shattered by her rejection of him, he ordered her slain. He watched as guards marched her to the chopping block, but hid his face in his hands as her head fell. Stumbling away, propped by an aide, he screamed further orders for the beheading of her mother, his sister's traitorous new husband, Castobar, and several other palace minions. He had plunged to the last edge of his own life.

Of Mariamne, Josephus writes: "A woman of great beauty and of excellent character, both for her chastity and greatness of soul." Once she was dead, "the king's affections for her were kindled in a more outrageous manner than before."

He frequently would call for her, and then imagining her present, he would talk regularly with her through long hours of the night as if she were still alive. All the while, the panic and delusions that had destroyed his only love continued to rear new terrors around him, including fear of his own sons and of the children of Bethlehem.

Once, as a young man on a hunt, Herod had fallen from his horse and been attacked by his own bloodthirsty hounds, eager for the kill. Flat on the ground, their foam-flinging jaws thrusting down on him, he had fought them off, killing several.

However, he still kept a pack of the hounds around him, always wary of them ever since that frenzied attack even though they normally groveled before him. In the same way, he was wary of life itself, dubious of its most intimate ties, unable to distinguish its blessings from its betrayals, or a lie from the truth. Slowly he was going mad.

3.
The Builder and Despoiler

The king's *curiosi*—his pervasive web of spies and informers that entwined the land—watched as the ten dagger-carrying assassins stationed themselves in the bawdy theater of Jerusalem, ready to die in their objective: the slaying of Herod the Great. His same ubiquitous "eyes" observed the scholars from the distant east as they entered the city, hunting a newborn king.

The vigilant sentinels also reported it when forty devout men mounted the Temple wall to tear down the Roman eagles.

In each case, mass reprisals struck in Judea. This

was the habitual response of a sick and volcanic King Herod.

"He was now overrun with suspicion and hatred against all about him," writes Josephus. "He encompassed the whole nation with guards, that it might by no means get from under his power."

At the same time he masked his oppression with extravagant building projects, savage sports, and perpetual levees—Roman style banquets that lasted far into the night with boisterous revelry.

Although biblical accounts scarcely mention it, the country at the time of Jesus' birth had been flooded with Greco-Roman practices and structures—public steam baths, theaters, fortresses, and hippodromes. The stadiums at Jerusalem, Jericho, and Caesarea resounded with the drill of troops, the screams of prisoners under torture, and the roar of crowds as gladiators battled, chariots raced and ravenous beasts leaped on condemned slaves or other victims.

These were the spectacular works of Herod who had initiated celebration of Olympian games every fifth year in honor of Caesar. Alien throngs swarmed to the city for the affairs, along with wrestlers, swordsmen, animal trainers, jugglers, and dancers. "Truly, foreigners were greatly surprised and delighted at the vastness of expenses here exhibited, and the great dangers that were seen," says Josephus, adding that the bloodletting horrified faithful Jews as barefaced impiety."

Ten precursors of the fanatic Sicarri, who were so named for the curved blades they carried under their cloaks and who had vowed vengeance against collaborators with Rome, posted themselves in the Jerusalem theater intending to assassinate Herod.

However, an informer warned him and Herod withdrew to his palace, sending his Galatian guards to seize the culprits. Confronting him, they boldly admitted their plan, calling it an holy action in defense of their faith.

"Thou hast despoiled the nation," they declared, "and transgressed its customs and laws of God, which all Jews are obliged to observe, or to die for them."

Herod had the men stretched on the rack until they perished. In the meantime, outraged citizens ambushed the king's hired spy and slew him in the street, tearing him limb from limb. Herod rounded up hundreds of witnesses, torturing them to learn the perpetrators, but without avail. Finally some women, shrieking in agony, blurted out the names. Herod seized and executed them along with their entire families.

Abouth this time of 7 B.C., (the likely birth date of Jesus despite subsequent miscalculations in forming the calendar), Herod's two sons by Mariamne, Alexander and Aristobulus, returned home from their education in Rome. Their presence aroused new trepidations in Herod's household. Tales came to him of their wrath at being "forced to live with those who had been their mother's murderers, and to be partakers with them."

Like a deadly, spreading vine, the tentacles of conspiracy and dread crept through Herod's new palace, which was built high on the western hill of Jerusalem's upper city. A tall Tower of Mariamne had been reared near its entrance. But it was full of terror and trouble. Herod could trust nobody.

Already afflicted with sundry physical maladies and tormented by nightmares that caused him to rave in his sleep, he had sought to smother his lurking fears in a splurge of exorbitant public construction and largesse. Over a ten-year period, he had rebuilt the Jewish Temple, using 10,000 stonecutters, carpenters, masons and 1,000 wagons to haul stone from ports and quarries and timber from the north. The magnificent edifice, its alabaster spires, white marble walls and Corinthian colonnades soaring atop Mount Moriah on the city's eastern side, was virtually complete at the time of Jesus' birth. It delighted the Jewish populace.

Herod's "atonement," the rabbis said, "for having

slain so many sages of Israel." Moreover, in the midst of two famines caused by severe droughts, he had brought wheat and corn—4,000 cori (equal to 55 gallons each)—from Egypt and organized bakers to process it to feed the starving.

Chiefly, however, he catered to his Roman masters, erecting costly temples and statues to their gods and Augustus Caesar in numerous outlying cities of his kingdom and in others abroad. Draining rich and poor alike for his royal treasury, he built a temple to Apollo at Rhodes, cloisters in Antioch and established imperial shrines, baths, and customs at Sapphoris on the Sea of Galilee, in surrounding cities of Perea—Ashkelon, Ptolemais, Scythopolis—and in Samaria and along the coasts of Judea.

At Caesarea, he raised a giant colossus equal to that of Jupiter in Rome, dedicated to Caesar, and also an amphitheater and an ingeniously engineered artificial harbor of circular stone breakwaters, bordered by a paved wharf and promenade, remains of which still stand today. He built another coliseum for combat, music, and sport in Sebaste northeast of Jerusalem; a second royal palace and stadium in Jericho; a chain of hilltop fortresses, including Masada and Machaerus near the Dead Sea; and Herodium on a hill shaped like a woman's breast overlooking Bethlehem.

As headquarters for his legions, he rebuilt the fortress Antonia in Jerusalem, named for his one-time Roman ally, Mark Antony, with underground passages connecting it with the new Jewish Temple.

Over his entire domain, across the heartland of Abraham, Jacob, David, and the prophets he drew the all-engulfing shadow of the Roman eagle. "The great mother of harlots and of the earth's abominations," the Book of Revelation calls it.

It dominated the civilized earth, its chalky, convex stone roads deploying its legions across thirty conquered provinces and bringing in a flow of tribute.

Ruling Romans paid no tribute—this was imposed only as an obligation to the master race, the *Imperium Mundi* of Caesar Augustus.

It was a coercive, suppressive society, of technical and artistic skill, but with no heart, no concern about individual abuse, or the trampling of the poor who were reckoned much as livestock for gain or sport in the arena. More than a third of the 54 million people of the empire—a million in Judea—were slaves. They were captives of war who were sold naked at auctions to toil in mines and building works with no rights, no claims even to their own young, knowing only the grim routine of rags, crusts, sweat, and lashings. As many as 150,000 war prisoners went on the slave market at one time, handled by professional dealers. Slaves could be killed or castrated without legal orders. Cripples sometimes were offered as sacrifices to the gods.

Girl slaves were sold into the highly organized prostitution business, rooted in the widespread fertility rites. The Temple of Aphrodite at Corinth had more than 1,000 sacred prostitutes for paying devotees.

Children, even of free men, could be sold like chattel, often under compulsion for debts or taxes. If unwanted, they were thrown out to die, a frequent practice with female babies. Judaism alone rejected infanticide. Onerous taxes reduced the poor to destitution, with levies on births, deaths, property, deeds, purchases, inheritances, merchandise sales, exports, imports, and an imperial poll tax, the *tributum* on every householder. It was such a tax census that brought Joseph and Mary to Bethlehem.

Under the overall supervision of an official in Rome called the Censor, collection of taxes was farmed out by bid on five-year contracts to provincial companies, the *publicani,* in which the wealthy in Rome owned shares.

Throughout the empire, official punishments were brutal—beheading, burning, the rack, cutting off ears and noses, stabbing out the eyes, and dragging through the streets. The harshest punishment of all, crucifixion was meted out to criminal slaves and insurrectionists against the empire. Prisoners could rot in their cells, since it was entirely up to magistrates when cases were brought for trial. King Herod, however, omitted trials altogether, blaring out his own frenetic verdicts.

At the Royal Portico of the Jerusalem Temple, those forty men led by two honored Jewish scholars, Judas and Matthias, had used ladders and ropes from the upper parapets to reach the eagle emblem mounted above the double entrance. In bright midday, at the sixth hour, they ripped down the hated image forbidden by their Scriptures, and cut it to pieces with axes. Word of the deed speedily reached Herod and guards brought the forty before him, their arms bound.

"Superstitious fools!" he bellowed. "Darest thou to destroy the ensign of Caesar?"

"Yes," the two rabbis said. "What was contrived we contrived, and what hath been performed we performed it, and those with us have acted with such courage as becomes men, in dedication to the majesty of Almighty God. Accordingly, we will undergo death or whatever punishment thou canst inflict upon us with pleasure since we are conscious that we shall die not for any unrighteous actions but for love of our religion."

Herod, his veined face flushed, a throbbing pain in the back of his head and ulcers tearing at his innards, ordered the two rabbis burned alive and the rest beheaded.

About that time, his household crawling with fears, hostilities, and machinations, Herod came into possession of a letter signed by his son, Alexander. Intended to taunt him, it read:

"You do not need to torture any more persons, for I have plotted against thee, and have many partners in it. So hast thy sister, Salome, who came to me by night and lay with me whether I would or not. All men are come to be of one mind, to make away with you, so as to get rid of the continual fear they are in from you."

Also at that time, spies informed Herod of the philosophers from the east, the Magi, inquiring about the city, "Where is he who has been born king of the Jews? For we have seen his star in the East, and have come to worship him."

Haggard, wild-eyed, roaring commands, Herod launched a new wave of arrests, including 200 officers associated with his son, and he ordered the Magi brought before him.

4.
Illness, Madness, and Magi

In a slow, steady rhythm, the barechested slaves swung the long fans of peacock feathers above King Herod's head, keeping off the flies. He sat propped on pillows, paring an apple, mouthing it off the blade. His hands shook. His breath came haltingly, in short gasps. Warily, his red-lined eyes shifted about the reception hall, scrutinizing the Syrian cooks with their laden platters, the rigid bodyguards, spears at their

sides, the dusky hounds sprawling on the tessellated
floor. Thin wisps of smoke curled from the three-legged
engraved brazier. A waterclock dripped monotonously.

Outside, along the covered pergola, he heard sand-
aled footsteps, and at once a sentry stepped through
the doorway drapes to announce the presence of the
eastern travelers.

King Herod watched with canny eyes as the be-
jeweled curtains parted and the three eastern philosophers were ushered before him.

They bowed in their accustomed manner, stretching
forth their hands at knee level. After an exchange of
amenities, Herod leaned forward, entwining his veined
fingers. Perspiration beaded his forehead as he spoke:
"Ye have spoken in the shops and streets of a new
kingly son," he said, "yet there has been no issue of
late in this household." He smiled grimly. "I can well
vouchsafe for that."

Then he leaned forward, and in confidential tones,
inquired at what time the star had appeared, for this
would determine the moment of nativity, and the present age of the child. "At what time, my astute doctors,
did you observe this *astar theios*—this divine star?"

The Magi, whether they realized it or not, were in a
precarious position. Their report of a newborn prince
had stirred up all Jerusalem, and caused consternation
among authorities.

Knowing Herod's blood-letting habits, they must
have stood there white and rigid as he demanded they
give details of the prophesied Christ. What do the
books say? Where is this God-king supposed to be
born?

"In Bethlehem of Judea," a quaking counselor had
said. "For thus it is written by the prophet: 'And thou
Bethlehem art not the least among the princes of
Judah: for out of thee shall come a governor, that shall
rule my people Israel.' "

So nervous had the man been that he somewhat mis-

quoted the prophet Micah who had written 700 years
before:

"But thou, Bethlehem, though thou be little among
the thousands of Judah, yet out of thee shall he come
forth that is to be ruler in Israel; Whose goings forth
have been from of old, from everlasting. . . . And he
shall . . . be great unto the ends of the earth. And this
man shall be the peace."

In any case, Herod, after ascertaining the geograph-
ical locale foreseen for the event, turned his attention
to the Magi, the Persian interlopers who had rekindled
the whole business.

What steps should he take? To execute them could
bring grave political repercussions, for they held royal
rank, and carried "safe conduct" tablets from Persia's
bellicose Parthian ruler, Phraates IV.

Next to the Romans, the Parthians were the world's
hautiest military power. Their famed horsemen and
archers could shoot unerringly even while moving, and
had overwhelmed many an elite corps in showers of
missiles. Phraates himself had trounced Mark Antony
and shattered his Roman infantry early in Herod's
reign. Since then, the emperor Augustus had come to
to terms with Phraates and they had exchanged tokens
of peace. Herod, whose crown depended on Augustus,
could not risk offending this accord. But possibly, if
he could not safely have the Magians strangled or
boiled in oil, he could use them—to his own ends.
After all, they were a widely venerated, priestly intelli-
gentsia, said to possess amazing talents. The king could
use some of his wit to wipe out this Bethlehem non-
sense.

"Go and search diligently for the young child," Herod
said ingratiatingly, "and when you have found him,
bring me word again, that I may come and worship
him." With these words the Magi departed, dubious
about Herod's intent, but nevertheless with freshened
certainty that they neared their objective.

Herod settled back in his seat, his eyes waxen, his thumb stroking the knife edge as the visitors disappeared through the damask curtains. The child would be under two, Herod calculated. He muttered to himself, reaching for a slab of roasted venison on a sidestand. He swallowed several bites and threw the rest to the hounds. They gulped it down and stood there, tongues lolling, greedy for more.

"Jackals, parasites, demons." He screamed at them as if they represented the world around him, ready to pounce. "Mariamne," he murmured, his head sagging. "Bring her! Bring her . . . my Mariamne!"

Then he gorged himself on more food, trying to soothe the ulcers scalding his insides. He also suffered from dropsy, fevers, convulsions, fierce head pains, a burning body rash, and festering tumors on his abdomen and feet. The glandular abnormalities and ulcers produced a ravening appetite and his gluttony only worsened the infections. He had difficulty breathing, and as the surplus liquids clogged his lungs, could do so only by sitting upright.

There was an odor about him, a foulness of breath. And his mind reeled with guilts, horrors and delusions, imagining his own sons swooping down on him, swords in hand, his murdered wife Mariamne wailing in the night, his guards abandoning him, the hounds at his throat.

At the urging of physicians, he spent long hours in the hot baths of Callirrhoe on the Dead Sea, and then had more baths in warm oil at his palace. But the medications gave only temporary relief and his disorders increased.

Occasionally he broke into wild lamentations about friends he had doomed at random, and then in opposite fashion, he would rage violently against them. At the same time, his unabated investigations and enveloping espionage system kept whetting rumors of treachery by his sons, Alexander and Aristobulus. At one point,

Herod put them on trial before Caesar Augustus while the emperor was on a visit in Beirut. He effected a reconciliation.

But his rival son, Antipater, continued to revive suspicions against the two. Herod had 200 courtiers confined for questioning. Some died from the lash, refusing to confess anything. But two tall, muscular guards, Jacundus and Tyrannus, who often had ridden with Alexander after Herod cast them off, confessed under torture that his son wanted them to kill the king and to say afterward that Herod had fallen on his own sword.

Adding to Herod's mounting alarms, his barber, Trypho, whispered to him that an old soldier, Tero, who had served with Herod in past wars, had urged the barber—in Alexander's behalf—to slit the king's throat while trimming his beard, a task the barber at that moment was performing. Herod, whipping off the apron spread over him, lunged to his feet, shouted for his Galatian guards to lock the barber in irons and also the old comrade-at-arms, Tero, and Tero's son.

In his hysteria, he ordered them all beheaded and also the 200 officers then in custody. As for Alexander and Aristobulus, he had them bound and taken to his fortified palace in Sebaste and strangled to death.

That was the last of them, as the deranged Herod counted it, the end of the royal Jewish clan that had beset and badgered him from the start, threatened and fought him, slandered his own ancestry, the last of that impudent, unmanageable brood. Finally, he gloated, he had purged his kingdom of them, exterminated them all, his challengers, his comrades . . . his cherished Mariamne . . . his own sons and hers.

However, a still nobler prince of David's line now tented in that realm, an infant named Jesus. Trembling, his sagging body dry with fevers and inflamed with itching, Herod threw off his clothes and shut himself in the steaming palace tepidarium, demanding oils, unguents, toweling the strigilis on his back. In no orderly sequence, he gulped down milk and tonics and railed incoherently at frightened slaves. He staggered to his bed, calling for powders on his flesh, choking for breath when he tried to lie down. Perspiring and clammy now, he huddled under downy quilts in a chair, his sensibilities drained, oblivious at one moment and starkly alert the next, then drooping off again into blurred vacuity.

Through watery eyes, he recognized the hounds at his feet, gape-mouthed, jowels dripping, mocking him. And then he realized he was staring into the face of his sister, Salome, who was warning him of further danger.

Had it not been Antipater who had first lodged the information against Mariamne's sons? True, true, he remembered, so it was, and Salome now had evidence that the case had been fabricated by deceit, forged confessions, and bribed accusers in a criminal alliance with Antipater.

Where was he? Where was Antipater? At the Herodium near the Dead Sea for the executions, Salome said. Herod lurched to his feet and bolted for the door, yelling for guards. Then he stopped stone still, realizing they already stood there, posted constantly in his chamber vestibule. He croaked the command to seize Antipater.

Shortly, he also received word that the Magi, those alien fomenters of treason, had tricked and outmaneuvered him. They had left the country secretly without leading him to the child.

"And, lo, the star, which they saw in the east, went before them, till it came and stood over where the young child was," Matthew's Gospel relates. "When they saw the star, they rejoiced with exceeding great joy."

It was a short, six-mile ride from Jerusalem south to Bethlehem. The house stood against a hillside. It was small, made of sun-hardened mud bricks. It had no windows. A narrow path led to the doorway, hung with a heavy wool cloth. Beside it leaned a woodsman's axe.

As the wayfarers approached, the only sound was the crunching of camel hooves on the red gravel. Melchior's lined face tensed. Neither he nor his two companions spoke. They stared ahead fixedly. This was the place. This was their goal. This was the star-touched habitation.

In front of the house, smoke curled from an earthen oven. A waterjar sat nearby, and a millstone. Off to one side of the house was a vegetable patch, and on the other, a little shed built against a Cypress tree. Wood shavings littered the ground beneath the open shelter, and on a work table lay knives, wedges, bow-drill, adze, mallet, and other carpenter's tools, along with some partly carved yokes and axles.

Travel-spent old Melchior held himself erect, his senses on edge. So here the long odyssey ended—in Bethlehem. He and the other Magi who had dedicated their minds, passions, and physical endurance to the dream of welcoming God's premier to mankind, stopped at last outside a peasant's hut.

Its occupants were not in sight.

The three stately callers slid to the ground. Servants, who had left their burros, took the reins of the camels, tapped their necks and pulled down on the halters, signaling them to kneel. Hastily, the Magians straightened their mantles. Melchior smoothed his long, white beard. Then he stepped to the doorpost. He caught his breath, and knocked. What answer lay within? What was its compelling power, its strange appeal?

It seemed odd, indeed, that the great eastern scholars should be there. They had wealth, prestige, acclaim. Yet there they stood, with pent-up solicitude, at the doorstep of an obscure Jewish family. What had engrossed them through the years? What had driven them across half a continent from Persia to this unlikely place?

The reason was plain to them. They saw, above all man's ambitions, attainments, and empires, the infinite logic of God. They believed he spoke a constant word to mankind in every evolving atom of the universe. And now, in this time and place, they sensed his most eloquent affirmation.

God had sent his Envoy. Truth had become flesh. The divine vocabulary was rendered in man's terms. God had bent down to man, and his voice rang out on earth.

The King had come!

The door covering was drawn aside, and the mild, steady gaze of Joseph met theirs. "What seek ye?"

"We seek one in whom God has visited in the person of a child."

Joseph surveyed the strangers fully, then bade them enter. "He is here."

The Magians filed through the doorway, Melchior hobbling in advance, followed by the grave, dark-skinned Balthazar, and then by Gaspar, young and beardless.

The floor was beaten clay with a sheepskin mat in the center and some low benches and utensils against the wall. In a corner, a shirt-clad infant played in a wooden crib. The quiet, young mother, Mary, picked him up, smiled faintly and sat down on a bench, displaying him on her knee. He was a year and some months of age. He looked up with wide-eyed interest at the visitors.

Melchior's lips parted wordlessly. Tears welled in his eyes. Then he and the others knelt on the dirt floor in reverence and worship. They had found their king. They had entered the presence of God's son.

There, in the ordinary beauty and innocence of a healthy toddler, God had provided his message to man.

How often the greatest truth is clothed in simplest array.

To recognize it required humility, the knowledge that knows its lack of knowledge. And this was the character of the Magi. While exalted scientists sought a world in space, they sought a world in time. They aspired, not to mere appearances, but to meanings. Through faith, they saw intuitively what others never see. Many see the stars. But who could see what the Magi saw? They saw the star of Bethlehem.

They beheld eternity in a twinkling. Truth, though everlasting, is revealed in a moment—and this was their moment of truth.

The child had been given the name *Yeshua,* or as the Greeks say, Jesus, which means "the salvation of Jehovah."

Presently, with joyous animation, the Magi hurried outside the house and brought forth gifts and laid them before him. Melchior presented gold, red gold, symbolizing a king's power. Gaspar brought myrrh, the seisin of burial and death, offering it with tears. Balthazar gave incense, the rich gum of Frankincense, signifying divine immortality.

Mary sat with bowed head, murmuring over each gift, "Thanks be to God."

Tradition says the royal Magi had brought huge coffers of pearls, silk hangings and other luxuries as intended presents, but so as not to offend the dignity of the poor, gave only what they first touched as they reached into their chests.

And so they left the humble abode as reverently as they came. Their misgivings about King Herod were intensified by ominous dreams. So they spurned his request to return to him and identify the child. Instead of taking the usual route home, northward through Jerusalem to Damascus, they went another way. Some accounts suggest they circled south toward Petra, crossing the copper-colored mountains of Moab.

Other reports say they slipped northward along the coast, departing by ship from the port of Tarsus in Cilicia, where Herod's troops, in vengeful pursuit, later wrecked the whole harbor.

The Magi also escaped back toward the rising sun, back to the elevated plateau of Persia, to the vineyards of Shiraz, back to the land of hornless cattle and poetry.

Some scholars say the Magi later built a chapel on Mt. Vaus, where they had first seen the star, and that they met there each year thereafter. They are said to have become bishops, ordained by the apostle Thomas.

After they died, their bodies were removed from Persia to Constantinople, then to Milan, and in 1163, to Cologne, where they now rest at the Cathedral of Cologne.

The Middle Ages claim that the Magi were kings, and they were, in a sense. They were sovereigns in the realm of wisdom, a royal heritage, beholden to its divine author. To average minds, their decision was folly. They acted with utter abandon. But despite the risks, the imponderables, and the distance, those who sought, found.

When Herod realized that he had been tricked, out-foxed, he went bellowing through the palace, alternately raging, weeping, and calling madly for his dead Mariamne. He descended to the dungeon cells and back again, searching the kitchens and storerooms, scattering the domestics in panic. He climbed again to the lofty ornate apartments and roof gardens in view of the tower named for her. Striking out with his scepter at wall hangings and jeweled furnishings, panting for air, at times falling to his hands and knees and crawling along the corridors like one of his hounds, he bellowed: "Mariamne . . . Mariamne!"

At one point, he grabbed a knife and tried to stab himself but a guard stopped him. He seemed not to

notice it or care. When Antipater was brought before
him, he pointed a wavering finger, bawling piteously.
"He would kill the king! Yet thou, O Antipater, was
the informer against my slain sons."

Death, he decreed for Antipater also. He ordered
troops to imprison all of the principal men of Jerusalem in the hippodrome just outside the city walls. He
directed that every soldier be paid an extra two-month
bonus, 50 drachmae, to keep them obedient. And he
dispatched a cohort of them to slay every male child
under two years of age in Bethlehem.

5.
Holocaust and Hope

Watching the princely camel train depart, Joseph
had a foreboding sense of uneasiness. There had been
only a hint, a veiled intimation, but it bore the trace of
terror. The child's life might be imperiled.

Joseph went back to his workbench and lifted a
piece of rough lumber to dress. From under it an adder
hissed and slithered away. Just then, a cloud crossed
the sun and brightness became shadow. Shrugging, he
proceeded with his work but the brooding disquiet
would not leave him. If danger threatened, he must act
to overcome it. He must not fail.

No one would harm that boy, no magistrate, no

court, nor legions of a vassal king! They would not touch a hair of him! The muscles of Joseph's large arms rippled and his beard dripped sweat as he planed the splintery board. It was strange how dark tidings often came sheathed in magnificent courtesies, so smooth so sensuous in such dignified decorum. Yet underneath they whisper of death.

Both he and Mary had been greatly awed by the visit of the Magi. Their gifts and obeisance to their child had been a wonder to behold.

Yet their arrival, after a journey of many months and 1500 miles, had stirred a commotion in nearby Jerusalem. The Magi had told of persistent inquiries about the child by Herod. However, they had given assurance that rather than going back through Jerusalem as Herod had requested, they would return by another way.

It was reassuring, yea, but also ominously unsettling. They already had revealed the place as Bethlehem. Joseph laid a dressed board on the heap and picked up another rough one to smooth and square. He could not shake off the nagging premonitions. He did not want to act rashly and without true cause. He did not want to frighten Mary and subject her and the child to needless hardship. A man must not be unnecessarily alarmed. He had to remain judicious, composed.

"A man of quick temper acts foolishly," his people's proverbs warned. "Keep sound wisdom and discretion. . . . Then you will walk on your way securely and your feet will not stumble. . . . Do not be afraid of sudden panic, or of the ruin of the wicked."

Yet the uneasiness remained. Thus far the child had thrived, learning to distinguish shapes and faces, to clasp with his fingers, his lips forming those untrained smiles that spring from some basic spark in human life. At more than one year of age, he was beginning to toddle about by bracing himself on walls or benches, and those first few words began to be uttered.

The family had remained through that period in Bethlehem. Galilee, their former home to the north, was still in a tumult of armed uprisings. Rebels roamed the countryside around Nazareth, and Roman troops struck and looted in the villages.

Joseph had found adequate work here in his ancestral town of Bethlehem. Mary and the child had been content. But now came this vague, new portent. It could be idle fancy or it could be deadly. He could not be sure.

After the evening meal, Joseph paced the house silently. Seeing Mary's concerned looks, he went outside and walked along an empty lane. He had to judge carefully, to discern, to know, to be ready.

Yet what could he, a poor, landless woodworker, do against the might of a king? Nonetheless, the charge was his. He clenched his big, callous hands before him, glaring into the night.

"O God," his heart cried with the psalmist, "when I am afraid, I put my trust in thee. Thy faithfulness is a shield and buckler. Delier my feet from falling."

That night, in the recesses of a dream, out of that hidden reservoir of understanding from which Joseph often had drawn insight and decision, an angelic vision appeared to him, saying: "Rise, take the child and his mother, and flee to Egypt, and remain there till I tell you; for Herod is about to search for the child, to destroy him."

In the middle of the night, Joseph arose from his bed of rushes. He awakened Mary and in quick, hushed tones, told her they must go. Pack only what can be carried in haste. Hurrying, he brought the burro from the field. He loaded the animal in the dark, his hands skilled to balance and touch, he distributed the utensils and his tools evenly on either side and folded a tent on top for a seat, girding the load with two straps.

The child was cradled in a sack slung on the burro's side. Joseph lifted Mary atop the level pack. He shouldered a sack of barley bread, cheese, dried fish, cucumbers and a goatskin of water and they slipped silently through the sleeping town and into the open country. Southward stretched the hills of Beersheba, the barren desert of Sinai, and finally, Egypt. It would be a far and lonesome road for Mary, the child, and for him.

The pale riders swung out of Jerusalem's fountain gate at daybreak and took the road south, descending along the Kidron valley and then winding back up the heights again toward Bethlehem. Their armor rattled. Hoofbeats drummed a rough tattoo. The tramp of many boots on the chalky stone stirred up an ashen pall of dust.

A tribune in plume-crested helmet rode at the head of a company of cavalrymen, followed by three chariots, their wheels mounted with scythes, and a cohort of 600 foot soldiers, equipped for combat. But there were muttered oaths and grumbling among them. They were on a mission of inhumane proportions. And even the strongest had to fight back a revulsion at what lay ahead.

The tribune's grip tightened on his lance, held erect in its fitting. Beside him rode the standard-bearer with the eagle emblem, and the trumpeter. He glanced back at the rest of his troops. Their bronze helmets, with the elaborate cheek pieces and the polished strips of their vest-like cuirasses, glittered in the sun. They also wore metal greaves fastened to their legs with thongs. Leather shields, affixed to wooden frames, swung from their shoulders.

The detachment included archers, javelin throwers and swordsmen who also carried battleaxes. They were part of the 12th legion garrisoned at Fort Antony. The 12th was one of twenty-eight legions of 168,000 men, mostly assorted mercenaries, that policed the empire's thirty provinces from Spain to the Arabian Sea.

Herod had four Roman legions of 24,000 men—the

3rd, 6th, 10th, and 12th—made up largely of Germans, Gauls, Tracians, and Samaritans to keep the insurgent Judean territory under control.

It was about fifty stadia (six miles) from Jerusalem to Bethlehem. As the cohort progressed, the tribune left his forward post and rode back along the line of march, checking it, taking the salutes of the centurions in their cape-like orange sagums. Swinging their vitus staffs of command, one centurion strode alongside each of the six centuries of footmen.

The tribune reached the rear echelon and spun about, galloping back to his forward position. The outfit seemed in order and ready, though a bit sullen, he thought. The assignment wouldn't take long nor involve any real danger. Yet it would be an unpleasant affair. He didn't want the use of the customary punishments inflicted on invaded cities—the pillaging, the taking of captives, the mutilation of male citizens, the impaling of heads or disemboweling of pregnant women. The orders simply were to exterminate the male youngsters.

He doubted that it would make much splash in the chronicles of Roman triumphs. No historian likely would even mention it. There were more spectacular blood-lettings to record in this recalcitrant province, particularly under the ruthless Herod. The Jews themselves were a strange people, insisting on one all-inclusive God, spurning any others.

As for the tribune's men, most of the Roman legionaries worshiped the dagger-wielding sun god, Mithra, and belonged to *Sol Invictus,* a cult for men whose weekly "Sun Day" rituals were observed in underground chapels. The altars showed relief works of Mithra, the bullslayer, his dagger driven into a prone bull, while dogs, serpents, birds and other animals drank the victim's blood and a scorpion clutched its genitals. The god's legendary birthday, December 25, was celebrated in the annual Saturnalia, a gaudy, ribald extravaganza in Rome and much of the empire—a feast that later would be taken over and observed as the birthday of the child whom the followers of Mithra marched to kill.

The tribune wet his lips, feeling the dust between his teeth. He wondered, would the Jewish belief in one just God have offered any better way? Under the present imperial religion, the innumerable gods were as capricious and brawling as human beings, with similar vanities, deceits, and rivalries, offering no clear standards of compassion, mutual responsibility, or peace among men. So the leeching of the defenseless went on unchallenged, and the debaucheries and perversions flourished in the cloisters of Ishtar.

At a three-way crossroads, where the main branch cut westward to Tekoa, another to the south, and a lesser road wound up the hill to Bethlehem, the tribune halted.

The town of about 5,000 stood on a ridge, 2,350 feet above sea level. In Jewish lore, it was the place where the Moabite girl, Ruth, pledged her loyalty to a native Jewish husband, Boaz. It was the place where the shepherd David tended his sheep and where the prophet Samuel anointed him king. It was a history-laden place for these sons of David. They were a peculiar people, overrun and dominated successively by Assyrians, Babylonians, Egyptians, Macedonians, and now Romans, yet still with an implacable passion for liberty and their comprehensive God of justice, they stubbornly believed that the righteous would at length inherit the earth.

But it didn't appear to be so at this point. Off to the side of the town stood one of Herod's impressive fortresses, encircled by round towers, its massive portcullis approached by a gleaming stairway of 200 polished stone steps. To the east, a broad gentle hillside sloped down into Shepherd's Field where sheepskin-cloaked herdsmen, armed with their rods and slings watched over their flocks by day and night.

In the stillness, the tribune could hear the high, sweet notes of their reed pipes. It was told that these shepherds first circulated word of the birth of this child of hope that frightens the king. Curiously, there at the crossroads also stood a stone pillar, marking the tomb of Rachel, the beloved wife of Jacob.

The tribune summoned his officers and gave them their final orders. The cohort would split into three sections, two centuries in each, moving in from three sides of the town, spearmen in advance. The cavalrymen and charioteers would remain in reserve. The mission was specific and restrictive—to destroy only males under two. The troops must judge the ages themselves. But let none escape. Heed no pleas or tears. There will be no spoils, no looting. Attend only to the limited objective—speedily, decisively, professionally—in the service of Caesar.

"Shall we decapitate them or dash them to pieces?" a centurion asked.

"Whichever is most expedient, or simply run them through. That should be sufficient. But make certain they're dead. If you encounter troublesome opposition, have a bowman put up a fireball. I'll be observing from up there." He pointed to a nearby hilltop.

The officers returned to their units and deployed their separate sectors as the column moved up the slope. The tribune, with the horsemen and chariots, headed to their vantage point on a hill beside the town. He planted the ensign there and watched. The silence hung heavily as the three wings of footmen closed in on the town. Then came the faint, desperate screams borne on the breeze, swelling to a steady, piercing wail.

It was as if these haunting words, attributed by the Jews to one of their prophets, echoed from that tomb down there. "A voice was heard in Ramah, wailing and loud lamentation, Rachel weeping for her children; she refused to be consoled, because they were no more."

Mary and Joseph avoided the main route, hiding by day and moving by night, watchful against pursuit. They circled towns where Roman troops might be posted, keeping to remote trails. They passed by Hebron, through the lonely reaches of Beersheba, and beyond the borders of Daroma into the desert with no trees for shade and where the wind heaved the sand into strange shapes, abutments, and caves. Mary sat on the donkey, shielding the child's eyes from the smiting sun.

As each day ended, the flaming sunsets seemed to send their fire licking along the very sand. Then the cold night would close down in sudden blackness, and Joseph would give his cloak to wrap the child. Their supply of bread hardened, their cheese and fish ran out. They ate shriveled cucumbers and hard bread while the burro grazed on thistles. The child, still a nursling until the age of two, rocked healthily in his sling.

As the distance lengthened, Joseph and Mary traveled by daylight, mingling with wayfarers, resting at watering places, camping at night among bedouins with their bright-striped tents and spirited horses. Along the roads were camels laden with casks of honey and bags of wheat, lines of slaves in leg-irons, driven by whips of their overseers. Joseph and Mary kept going, footsore, sunscorched, weary, wiping the dust from the face of the child they loved.

They were in Egypt now, a country of showily displayed idolatry, of monuments and shrines to animal-like gods—the ox, the cat, the crocodile. In alien towns, Joseph replenished their foodstuffs. They crossed the Nile on a ferry raft propelled by poles. In the distance loomed the giant pyramids, built by toiling armies of slaves in bondage to Pharaoh—as the forebears of Joseph and Mary once had been.

Artists have portrayed the small boy, Jesus, sleeping in his mother's arms between the massive paws of the

Sphinx. According to ancient, noncanonical writings, the family lived for a time at Heliopolis, where a small Jewish community existed.

Largely, however, the accounts say, they were driven by circumstances from place to place, once living in a lean-to shack built by wattles against a ruined wall, at times finding shelter on steps or in an archway, sharing the space with beggars, the maimed, and orphaned waifs. They were refugees, impoverished strangers in a strange land, without friends, ignorant of the language. Joseph knocked on many doors, gesturing with his tools to make known he sought work. He frequented the marketplaces where contractors hired labor crews, and took backbreaking jobs, cutting rocks and hauling them on huge, wheeled platforms.

The old nonbiblical accounts say they encountered thieves, sorcerers, a pathetic mad woman who stripped herself naked, and aided a woman attacked by serpents. Mary did her washing in springs and rivers. Occasionally, admiring strangers lifted up the boy Jesus to embrace him.

It was a period of wandering loneliness, of rejection, isolation, and hardship. Some ancient writings suggest it lasted seven years; others say it was only a matter of months. However, since Jesus was born about three years before Herod's death, and was more than a year old when Joseph fled with him, they evidently had to remain in exile about two years—until after Herod's death.

When the blood-smeared troops returned, they brought word of a couple that, reportedly, had fled to Egypt—a carpenter, his wife, and a small child named Yeshua, meaning the "Salvation of God." The information was relayed to the dying Herod, rapidly disintegrating from the ravaging intestinal ulcers which had become cancerous, from the edema drowning his

flesh in purulent matter, and from his maniacal delu-
sion of persecution.

"I shall die without being lamented," he groaned.
"The Jews will make a festival upon my death. But
I have the power to compel them to mourn at it, on
whatever account, as befits a king."

To insure it, he ordered the city's chief Jewish noblemen, already confined in the hippodrome, to be slain
by archers stationed around the arena immediately
upon the king's death. Also, legionnaires were put
under orders to kill—at the same time—one member
of each native family. "Then all Judea and every family
of them, will weep at my death, whether they will
or not," he said, panting for breath, his eyes opaque
and staring.

He died screaming in 4 B.C. at the age of seventy.
His death took place in Jericho, the hounds that pursued him still at his bedside. "A man he was of great
barbarity to all men equally," wrote Josephus. "He
stole the throne like a fox, ruled like a tiger and died
like a dog."

His will bestowed 10 million drachmae and vessels
of gold and silver on Augustus Caesar, and divided his
kingdom among three sons, Antipas, Philip, and Archelaus, survivors among the ten sons and five daughters
of his ten wives. He had slain five sons, including those
of his only love, Mariamne, whom he also killed.

His body, arrayed in purple, the diadem on his
head, his scepter in his hand, was laid on a golden bier,
embroidered with precious stones, and bourne thirty
miles from Jericho through Jerusalem to his fortified
citadel, Herodium, overlooking Bethlehem, for his
burial. The procession included 500 slaves, his Galatian bodyguards, and a Roman cohort in battle re-
galia.

But his final order for more carnage was ignored.
He was not even mourned by Augustus, who once
called him "confederate and friend," but who in the

end remarked, "Better to have been Herod's hogs than his sons."

The king, the empire, the far-spread domain of mighty legions and the glories and gods of the world had sought to stamp out a spark of sheer goodness that entered into the night of that age. However, the light burned on, greater than all the panoplies of Caesar, waxing ever stronger amid the dangers of earth, freeing, healing, and heartening, despite unending onslaughts against it.

Ironically, Bethlehem—the place where Herod the Great first tried in vain to extinguish that Christmas light—marks his own grave.

Once again, as so often before, Joseph found his guidance in a dream. "Rise, take the child and his mother, and go to the land of Israel, for those who sought the child's life are dead."

The long flight was over. Some legends say they returned by ship, boarding at Alexandria. By whatever means, they journeyed back to Israel. They intended to return to Bethlehem, but learned that Archelaus, a murderous son of Herod, now ruled there, and 2,000 Jews had been crucified; 3,000 slain in riots; and 30,000 sold into slavery.

To safeguard his family, Joseph changed their course and destination. He led them along the western sea coast northward into the fertile valleys and mountains of Galilee. Back to Nazareth. They had been fugitives, struggling migrants, homeless in alien surroundings for two years, the child condemned to death by a king. But he was saved by the canny, resolute Joseph.

The prophet Hosea long before had heralded God's intent: "Out of Egypt I have called my son." And it was the sturdy Joseph who preserved the boy through that grim ordeal and brought him safely home.

PART 2
The Precursors

1.
The Early Questioners

From the start, a difficult question beat at the heart
of the world. Who owns it? And for what intent? "What
is his name?" puzzled Moses more than 3,200 years
ago while his enslaved people toiled under the Egyptian
oppressor, Pharaoh Ramses II. To whom, or what,
does man belong? Where lies his authentic allegiance?

The answer remained searingly elusive, unbound to
manageable equations or definitions. "I AM WHO I
AM." That was about the only inkling Moses got at
first. It was mystifying, the central enigma. Whence
came this cosmos, this life, and whither?

But clues accumulated through time and events,
chiefly for Christians, in the birth of a Jew called
Jesus. But it wasn't an isolated occurrence. Jesus stood
in a long succession. He came in turn in the unfolding
of history's disclosures. He was part of a process. It
foreshadowed him. It pointed to him, before and
since. Its prior agents were the ancient prophets of
Israel.

They were the precursors who witnessed to him. He
said, "Everything written about me in the law . . .

and the prophets must be fulfilled." They prefigured what they termed the "elect one," the "anointed," the "Day of the Lord." They were a fiercely challenging phenomenon, among the most disturbing men ever known.

Like the one they preceded, they defied established systems. They were protesters, rebels, reformers, idealists in a groping, confused era. They emblazoned a lofty concept of man's role and right obligations. They were scorned, ridiculed, flogged, imprisoned, and sometimes killed. They were lonely, anguished men, often pursued as fugitives, marked as traitors.

"Get away from me!" the Egyptian monarch roared at the prophet Moses who had demanded liberation for his people from enslavement in 1290 B.C. "Take heed to yourself," the pharaoh warned, threatening him with death if he appeared again to press the issue. "For in the day you see my face you shall die." But Moses persisted.

And the people miraculously broke free of the grinding tyranny, giving them the first vivid, memorable impression of an ultimate sovereign allied with them, of a supreme deliverer, loosing them from their chains, redeeming them. "The Lord is my strength and my song, they sang, "and he has become my salvation."

The continuing line of prophets thundered that defense of human dignity, of help for the imprisoned, of strength for the downtrodden and abused, of hospitality to the stranger and alien, of peace among peoples and equity for every person. "Nabi," they were called, "speakers" or "announcers" of the divine will among men. They were not soothsayers or fortunetellers practicing occult arts, but they discerned keenly the shape of the times, its directions and impending consequences.

Neither were they mechanically speaking divine dictation. Rather, they were intensely conscientious men, sensitive to God's vision of the world, attuned to it, and conveying it through their own particular human perspective and temperaments. And they were continually appalled at the complacency of the proud and powerful. Unlike the temple-confined pagan religions, they saw divine concern as engaged with history, and they hurled their exhortations at kings, governments and social orders.

"You are the man!" the prophet Nathan blazed at the great King David, after telling him a story of a rich landlord who had seized a poor peasant's only sheep for a feast, leading David to sternly declare the rich man in the wrong. At that point, Nathan drove it home. "You are the man!" For the much-married David of about 1,000 B.C. also had taken for himself a soldier's only wife, Bathsheba.

Although the rulers sometimes had their own fawning circle of seers and prophets who served only to please their superiors and sanction official policy—as heirs of that role still do—the genuine truth-bearers, the real prophets, were ruggedly uncompromising.

"You troubler of Israel!" King Ahab flared at the prophet Elijah when that desert mystic, clad in hairskin and leather girdle, appeared about 860 B.C. to condemn the national idol worship of Baal and Astarte promoted by the queen Jezebel. Condemned, hunted, hiding near the end of his life in a cave, Elijah sorrowed that other prophets had been "slain by the sword, and I, even I only, am left, and they seek my life."

But others would arise after he vanished in a whirlwind, including his pupil Elisha, who also met jeers, even from young boys. "Baldhead, go up, you baldhead!" they taunted him.

These were agitated, indignant men, pained by the rampant greed, alarmed at the exploitation of the poor, passionately concerned for human welfare, as if they mirrored the very pathos of God at man's callousness. "Hear this, you who trample upon the needy!" declared the rural prophet Amos around 760 B.C. He was a

lowly tree-tender from Tekoa but he warned that divine
justice would "smite the capitals until the thresholds
shake" and "darken the earth in broad daylight" as a
result of the oppressions going on.

Fearless, acute, driven by some inner fire, the prophets flung their jolting admonitions at a flabby, delin-
quent society, and as happens in every age, it drew
stern reactions. Amos was charged with conspiracy.
"The land is not able to bear his words," agents reported to King Jeroboam II, whose crushing taxes bled
the impoverished farmers and enriched the riotous cult
of Meribaal.

As with other prophets, Amos' message was that a
universal Creator of the world is actively involved in
its affairs, interrelated with men and their institutions,
and that their right function is to advance human
betterment, not ritual posturing.

"Thus says the Lord God, I hate, I despise your
feasts, and I take no delight in your solemn assemblies,"
Amos proclaimed. "Take away from me the noise of
your songs; to the melody of your harps I will not
listen. But let justice roll down like waters, and righteousness like an everflowing stream."

Amid the confusion and decadence of the times,
however, the prophets also sensed an eventual rejuven-
ation, the sunburst of new clarity, cleansing and universal dominon wrought by a divine emissary, a re-
newing champion of humanity in whom Christians see
intimations of Jesus Christ.

The prophet Nathan told King David that God
would raise up a descendant and "establish the throne
of his kingdom for ever," that he would be God's own
son, chastened "with the stripes of the sons of men."
"And I will make him the first-born, the highest of
the kings of the earth," went Psalm 89, one of those
strangely futuristic psalms. "I will establish his line for
ever . . . it shall stand firm while the skies endure."

Even further back, in the misty story of creation

and man's sinful attempt to deify himself, a verse in Genesis 3:15 has been regarded as referring to a coming representative of the Creator who would counteract human corruption and "bruise" the head of the serpent, personifying evil. "The scepter shall not depart from Judah . . . until he comes to whom it belongs," goes another remote allusion in Genesis 49. "And to him shall be the obedience of the people. . . ."

"A star shall come forth out of Jacob," says an obscure oracle in Numbers 24, another part of the ancient Torah, or Pentateuch, often attributed to Moses. The early intimations were vague, often ambiguous, hazy prophetic visions of a coming divine intervention among men. "I will pass through the midst of you, says the Lord," wrote Amos, adding a brooding note that could refer to the ordeal of Jesus. "Woe to you who desire the day of the Lord! It is darkness and not light."

A description of the very scene that would involve Jesus on the cross hundreds of years later showed up in some ancient Davidic hymns, as recorded in Psalms 22: "My God, my God, why hast thou forsaken me? A company of evildoers encircles me; they have pierced my hands and feet . . . they divide my garments among them, and for my raiment they cast lots! Yea, to him shall all the proud of the earth bow down. Posterity shall serve him . . . and proclaim his deliverance to a people yet unborn, that he has wrought it."

2.
Isaiah

Scandalizing national policy, the barefoot, scantily clad demonstrators roamed the streets and plazas of Jerusalem, led by the learned prophet Isaiah, protesting an alliance for war. It was an ancient scene with modern counterparts.

Maher-Shalal-Hash-Baz, read a large parchment sign he carried, warning of precipitous ruin by arms. "Swift-Spoil-Speedy-Prey."

For three years, up to 711 B.C., this famed aristocratic sage of Judah had paraded about the city unshod and nearly naked, stripped to a loin strap, brazenly opposing the country's military coalition against the heathen Assyrian empire. "A covenant with death!" he called it.

"Draw near, O nations, to hear, and hearken, O peoples. Woe to those who trust in chariots because they are many and in horsemen because they are very strong. . . . Woe to you, destroyer. When you have ceased to destroy, you will be destroyed." Such stinging indictments eventually would bring official fury crashing down on the prophet.

It was a time of turmoil, conflict, and rising fear.

Faith shrank, justice tottered, and disorder grew. The rich plundered the poor and soldiers rushed about, shouting commands. "A city of chaos," Isaiah cried. But in the midst of the institutional deceit, pretensions, wealth, and overriding want, Isaiah saw glimmerings of future hope that later would be regarded as heralds of Jesus.

"The people who walked in darkness have seen a great light," the prophet said. "For to us a child is born, to us a son is given; and the government will be upon his shoulder, and his name will be called Wonderful, Counselor, Father, Prince of Peace. Of the increase of his government and of peace there will be no end."

Through the reigns of four kings, the nobly born, intellectually gifted Isaiah served as a royal counselor, goading the nation's conscience. His advice was sometimes heeded, sometimes scorned, and suppressed. He was a broadly endowed man, a piercing poet, an adept statesman, a man of action and public affairs, unabashed in the presence of rulers. He was distressed at the militarism and oppressions, luxury in the face of poverty, the perversions of justice—themes relevant to every age, including our own.

"Your princes are companions of thieves," he declared. They "acquit the guilty for a bribe, and deprive the innocent of his right." They "turn aside the needy from justice and rob the poor."

Considered the greatest of the Jewish prophets, Isaiah, like the others, never hesitated to bring politics into the pulpit. Government policies and social conditions were prime concerns—the imprisonments, the slavery, the official lies and corrupt courts, the exhorbitant tax levies, the bleeding of the poor. "Seek justice, correct oppression, defend the fatherless, plead for the widows," Isaiah urged in a ministry Jesus later cited as like his own. "Strengthen the weak hands, and make firm the feeble knees.

In the prophetic tradition, Isaiah was a watchman, a
guardian of the people's rights, a proclaimer of God's
loving aspirations for mankind, of divine participation
in human history and the inevitable tragedy resulting
from ignoring those providential goals. Like others of
that calling, he at first resisted, considering himself
unqualified. He had been kneeling in the Jerusalem
Temple, immersed in the atmosphere of prayer, incense, and trilling flutes when the divine assignment
seized him.

"Woe is me!" he moaned. "For I am lost; for I am
a man of unclean lips." Suddenly, a burning coal from
the high brass altar tumbled down, scorching his lips,
shooting through him a fiery reassurance of forgiveness
and acceptability, and then came his Makers searing
question:

"Who shall I send, and who will go for us?"

"Here I am!" He stood up, ready. "Send me."

He was in his early twenties then, a brilliant, well-to-
do young Jewish scholar, married to an alert, studious
wife. They had two sons. The time was 740 B.C., the
year Judah's King Uzziah died.

Thus began Isaiah's more than forty years of baring
the truth, of inveighing against arrogance and avarice,
pleading for peace and compassion. His mission lasted
through the reigns of Jotham, Ahaz, Hezekiah, and
probably the early years of Manasseh.

It was in the reign of the nervous, rabbity Ahaz,
who about 732 B.C. had planned a military pact with
the mighty Assyria, that Isaiah first spoke out against
such warlike combinations. "Do not fear . . . these
two smouldering stumps of firebrands," the prophet
told Ahaz, predicting their own armed threats would
be their downfall.

But Ahaz spurned the advice, shackling his country
to the overshadowing Assyria, paying it heavy tribute
which impoverished Judah, installing Assyria's pagan

rites, serpent images, and erecting altars to Astarte, Nergal, and to the human-headed bull-god of war.

Isaiah, in one of those strangely veiled premonitions, said that as a sign against Ahaz, a "young woman shall conceive and bear a son, and shall call his name Immanuel"—meaning "God with us." Judaism sees this as presaging an early reversal of Ahaz's entangling bid for domination by armed force, but many Christians regard it as a vision of the birth of Jesus, of the divine will become flesh, more than 700 years later. In fact, both happened.

Another prophet, Micah, from the village of Morsheth in the hills southwest of Jerusalem and a younger, peasant contemporary of the upperclass Isaiah, also foresaw a coming emissary of God, citing Bethlehem in the district of Ephrathah as his birthplace, the little town of Jesus' nativity.

"But you, O Bethlehem, Ephrathah, who are little to be among the clans of Judah, from you shall come forth one who is to be ruler in Israel, whose origin is from of old, from ancient days. . . . And he shall stand . . . in the majesty of the name of the Lord his God. . . . He shall be great to the ends of the earth."

Isaiah's strange intimations of holy opposition to Ahaz infuriated the king, who apparently ordered the prophet silenced, branding him a conspirator against the state. But Isaiah continued his work outside official circles, teaching his disciples and assembling his sermons in a book.

In the ensuing devastation which Isaiah had foreseen, Judah's new ally, the Assyrian war machine, crushed Syria in terrible carnage, slaying its king. Then in 722 B.C., Assyria destroyed the northern kingdom of Israel, enslaving its people, who vanished from history —the ten "lost tribes."

Hezekiah succeeded to Judah's throne in 716. Alarmed at the encircling depradations of Assyria, he revoked Ahaz's subservient policy, banished the alien idols, and plotted a new military compact wtih Egypt. Isaiah also condemned the new military alignment, which he termed seeking "shelter in the shadow of Egypt," as he had the previous alliance with Assyria. But Hezekiah went ahead with it, bolstering his armory and displaying his weapons.

Isaiah began his prolonged public protest, walking the streets daily in a state of undress, symbolizing the barrenness of "security" in armaments. It will "turn to your shame," he said, and God will use idolatrous Assyria itself as "the rod" of reprisal to shatter "the pride of the arrogant, and lay low the haughtiness of the ruthless."

Retaliating swiftly against Hezekiah's new pact, the Assyrian juggernaut under Sargon II rolled over Egypt, conquering it. Then under the brutal Sennacherib, it razed forty-six walled cities of Judah, dragging 200,150 people into slavery, and then brought its troops, catapults, and battering-rams to the capital, Jerusalem. The city was in panic.

"Ah, the thunder of many peoples, they thunder like the thundering of the sea," Isaiah observed. "Ah, the roar of nations, they roar like the roaring of mighty waters!"

The frightened population rushed about, gorging itself on remaining supplies. "Let us eat and drink," they said, "for tomorrow we die."

"All joy has reached its eventide," Isaiah said, yet he still clung to the image of a coming true representative of God's righteousness—"a shoot" from Jesse.

"And the Spirit of the Lord shall rest upon him, the spirit of wisdom and understanding. . . . With righteousness he shall judge the poor, and decide with equity for the meek of the earth. . . . Righteousness shall be the girdle of his waist, and faithfulness the girdle of his loins."

A frantic King Hezekiah, his city surrounded and helpless for all his military preparedness, turned at

last to earnest prayer, "O Lord our God, save us."
Then he summoned the stubborn protestor, Isaiah, and
asked what to do.

Assyria's forces, Isaiah said, "shall not come into
this city."

They didn't. That night, 185,000 of them fell fatally
ill with a fly-borne pestilence. The rest retreated in
disarray. Sennacherib was murdered by his sons. But
the ordeal wasn't over. Under the next king, Manasseh,
Judah was plunged into further decandence under
Assyrian vassalage, with its cruelties, heathenism, and
even human sacrifice. Tradition says the valiant critic,
Isaiah, was executed by being sawed apart.

But he left his radiant hope of a future divine scepter
on earth. "Behold, a king will reign in righteousness.
. . . And a highway shall be there . . . the holy way
. . . the redeemed shall walk there . . . the ransomed
of the Lord. . . ."

A transitional time would come in human history,
he said, and it would point ahead to a future of universal blessedness.

"For the earth shall be full of the knowledge of the
Lord as the waters cover the sea. In that day the root
of Jesse shall stand as an ensign to the peoples; him
shall the nations seek, and his dwellings shall be
glorious.

"He shall raise a signal. . . . He shall judge between the nations . . . and they shall beat their
swords into plowshares, and their spears into pruning
hooks; nation shall not lift up sword against nation,
neither shall they learn war anymore. . . .

"The wolf shall dwell with the lamb, and the leopard
shall lie down with the kid, and the calf and the lion
and the fatling together, and a little child shall lead
them."

3.
Jeremiah

Bruised, lacerated, and thigh-deep in mud at the bottom of an empty cistern, Jeremiah waited for the end. "They flung me alive into the pit . . . I am lost," says his Book of Lamentations.

The aged prophet had been beaten and dumped into the deep stone shaft to die about 588 B.C. for condemning slavery. He was charged with treason as a menace to national defense and security.

"Let this man be put to death, for he is weakening the hands of the soldiers," demanded the chauvinistic courtiers of Judah's King Zedekiah, who had ordered armed mobilization against the Babylonian forces of Chaldea.

That empire had become the world's new ominous colossus of the east in 612 B.C., crushing Assyria which had dominated the area for nearly a century, and in rapid order, making Egypt, Judah and other states subject to it.

For nearly forty years—through the vicissitudes of imperial domination over Judah, first by Assyria, then briefly by Egypt and now by Babylonia—Jeremiah had pleaded for internal moral and religious integrity as Judah's only hope for surmounting the maelstrom.

"Amend your ways and your doings," he urged, and the nation shall endure blessedly, but otherwise, it "shall become a desolation."

It was an appalling insight of self-destruction, but one that would apply down through history to sick societies plunging into oppression, fraud, ostentation, licentiousness and decay.

"Behold, evil is going forth from nation to nation, and a great tempest is stirring," the prophet said. "The clamor will resound to the ends of the earth, for the Lord has an indictment against the nations." His dire portents and attacks on prevailing conditions kept him in continual jeopardy.

"Denounce him!" yelled the mob patriots. "Let us denounce him."

As related in the books of Jeremiah and also II Kings, his writings were burned and he was repeatedly threatened with death, even by neighbors. At various times, he was imprisoned, flogged, pinioned publicly in stocks, forced into hiding, half buried in a well and eventually driven into exile. "We looked for peace," he said, "but no good came, for a time of healing; but behold, terror."

He was a lonely, solitary figure, unmarried, ostracized even by his relatives, sometimes even feeling cut off from the divine focus of his own life so that God seemed like a stranger. "O Lord, thou hast deceived me," he agonized at one point. "I have become a laughingstock . . . a reproach and derision all day long. Cursed be the day on which I was born!"

Yet if he considered abandoning his calling to declare God's way for man's fulfillment, he said there would come "in my heart as it were a burning fire shut up in my bones," and he could not hold it in. "My anguish, my anguish!" he exclaimed. "I cannot keep silent; for I hear the sound of the trumpet, the alarm

of war. Disaster follows on disaster, the whole land is
laid waste."

But even as he recognized the gathering clouds of
doom, he sensed the unshakable divine attachment to
humanity so keenly that he knew it must eventually
bring a reconciliation. "Behold the days are coming,
says the Lord, when I will make a new covenant with
the House of Israel and the House of Judah, not like
the old covenant. . . ." Jeremiah wrote in a passage
which Christians see as the coming of Jesus. "I will
put my law within them, and I will write it upon their
hearts . . . and no longer shall each man teach his
neighbor and each his brother, saying 'Know the Lord,'
for they shall all know me. . . . I will forgive their
iniquity and I will remember their sin no more."

That, however remote the allusion, was Christ's proclaimed purpose. To Jeremiah, the immediate lesson he
discerned was the inescapable damage wrought among
human beings by their derelictions.

"The storm of the Lord," he called it. But it was
not, as often misconstrued, the punishment of an
avenging God but rather the self-infliction of a race
out of touch with whole (holy) living and disaster-
bent because of it. "Hear this, O foolish and senseless
people, who have eyes but see not, who have ears, but
hear not," Jeremiah said. The Lord will pour out the
people's own "wickedness upon them."

"Those who are for pestilence, to pestilence, and
those who are for the sword, to the sword; those who
are for famine, to famine, and those who are for captivity, to captivity." The human scene would reap its
own choices. It was, as it always is for man, his own
option.

But openly declaring the hazards in a smugly rigid
environment could be costly, as Jeremiah found. "O
Lord, I did not sit in the company of merrymakers,
nor did I rejoice; I sat alone, because thy hand was

upon me, for thou hadst filled me with indignation."
Speaking the truth made living rough.

Jeremiah, son of a priest and member of the tribe of
Benjamin, came from the village of Anathoth about
two miles northeast of the capital of Jerusalem. When
he first became aware of his prophetic role, he complained. "Ah Lord God! Behold, I do not know how to
speak for I am only a youth." He was in his twenties.
But the divine summons overruled him. "Be not afraid
. . . for I am with you. . . ."

His ministry lasted from 626 to 580 B.C. in the back-
wash of the abominations left by the vile King Manasseh, who had been totally subservient to the Assyrians
and their barbarous paganism. Infant sacrifice, enforced slavery, and brutal iniquities infested Jerusalem.
There were also shrines to Ishtar, Nanar, Chemosh,
and other nature cults accompanied by their fetishes,
incantations, and ritual prostitution.

Denouncing the profligacy, the sorcerers, and idolatry, Jeremiah said the city was rotten with graft, ex-
tortion from the poor and innocent bloodshed, with the
ruling regime "heaping oppression upon oppression,
and deceit upon deceit."

As Assyria's influence declined, however, some religious reforms were briefly undertaken. These were
under King Josiah in 621 B.C. after the discovery of a
long-lost scroll of Jewish law, believed to have been
the ancient biblical Book of Deuteronomy. Jeremiah,
although commending the efforts, warned against mere
verbalized piety without action for social justice. "Do
not trust in these deceptive words: 'This is the Temple
of the Lord, the Temple of the Lord, the Temple of
the Lord. We are delivered!' " Rather, he said, the
people must "execute justice" in deed to purge the de-
graded environment if it were to survive.

However, the renewal impulse soon collapsed when
King Josiah was killed in the year 609 in a battle with
Egypt's forces. The Egyptian Pharaoh Necho dictated

Judah's next king Jehoiakim, an unscrupulous, grasping puppet, bringing back mass depravity.

"The harvest is past, the summer is ended, and we are not saved," Jeremiah grieved. "Is there no balm in Gilead? Is there no physician there?"

With a crowd of sympathizers, he staged a demonstration outside the city walls, breaking a clay flask into bits to dramatize the fate facing Jerusalem. Then, standing in the Temple inner court, he declared that Judah's debauchery would bring its destruction by Babylon.

Pashur, the priest-son of the Temple's chief security officer, had the prophet flogged and locked in stocks in the Benjamin gate as a public enemy. The fettered Jeremiah raged at his persecutor, "The Lord does not call your name Pashur, but 'Terror'."

Released the next day, Jeremiah continued his unrestrained criticisms, assailing Judah's military alliance with Egypt against Babylon. Officials seized him, "You shall die!" He was put on trial for treason. Another prophet, Uriah, already had been executed for similar warnings of a military catastrophe.

Jeremiah was let off temporarily under surveillance. Barred from the Temple precincts, he dictated a scathing sermon to his amanuensis, Baruch, and had him read it publicly. "Hark, a rumor! Behold, it comes! A great commotion out of the north country to make the cities of Judah a desolation."

Aides to King Jehoiakim seized the manuscript and delivered it to him. As he read the scroll, he took a penknife and cut off each section as he finished, and threw it into the brazier to burn. "Seize Baruch the secretary and Jeremiah the prophet," he ordered.

The pair fled into hiding, making another copy of the document. "Woe is me . . . a man of strife and contention to the whole land," Jeremiah sorrowed. "All of them curse me, waiting for my fall. But the Lord is with me as a dread warrior."

In 605 B.C., four years after Egypt overcame Judah,
Egypt itself was overwhelmed by Babylon in the Battle
of Carchemish, making Babylonia the master of the
middle east from the Nile to the Euphrates rivers.
When Judah's King Jehoiakim launched resistance
against the new conqueror, Jeremiah returned to warn
him that Judah would become "a horror, a hissing, an
everlasting reproach." Soon afterward, in 598, Babylon's forces invaded Jerusalem, sending its leading
artisans and king into captivity.

Jeremiah urged the newly installed ruler, Zedekiah,
to concentrate on peaceful social reform. "Do justice.
Deliver from the hand of the oppressor him who had
been robbed. And do no wrong or violence to the alien,
the fatherless and the widow, nor shed innocent blood."
Zedekiah wavered between pacification and new military operations, finally giving in to the hawkish war
planners. Jeremiah mourned, "They have healed the
wound of my people lightly, saying 'Peace, Peace,'
when there is no peace."

He was cast into a dungeon, but later removed to a
guard house on instructions of the king who continued
consulting him. When a royal order freeing Jerusalem's
slaves went unenforced and ignored, Jeremiah thundered: "Thus says the Lord: You have not obeyed me
by proclaiming liberty, everyone to his brother . . ." As
a result, he said, the country would be subjected to
sword, famine and the horror of Babylon's forces who
would "burn it with fire."

Soon afterward, with Babylon's troops pounding at
the walls and the city swept with hunger and panic,
Jeremiah was arrested again, once more accused of
treason, and with the king's approval, cast into the
empty cistern to starve.

"Terror is on every side," Jeremiah lamented. "O
daughter of my people, gird on sackcloth and roll in
ashes." He clung to a protruding rock in the cistern to
avoid sinking in the stagnant ooze. "My heart is broken

within me, all my bones shake. . . . I was led like a gentle lamb to the slaughter."

The deep bottle-shaped cistern, wide at the bottom, narrowed to a neck at the top, was covered with a stone slab. Below, fallen clay jars and broken pots littered the rancid mire, crawling with snakes and vipers. "O Lord! Thou has walled me about . . . besieged and enveloped me with bitterness and tribulation . . . made me to dwell in darkness like the dead. . . ."

But even in despair, Jeremiah saw a "future and a hope"—an expressed anticipation which Jews regard as a promise of national restoration and which Christians see as a harbinger of Jesus. "Thus says the Lord. In those days and at that time I will cause a Righteous Branch to spring forth for David; and he shall execute justice and righteousness."

The stone covering on the cistern was pushed aside and the light poured in. A black Ethiopian slave named Ebedmelech lowered ropes to Jeremiah and pulled him out.

Jerusalem was in its last throes. The prophet burst in to see the king and urged him to give up the battle. The king refused and sent Jeremiah back to prison. The city fell in 587 B.C. It was sacked and burned, and its people taken into captivity in Babylon for the next forty-nine years.

Jeremiah, an old man, was led in chains to Mispah in the north and later taken as a prisoner into exile in Egypt where he died, convinced that God is not "afar off" but "at hand," his "everlasting love" constantly bestowed on men to bring them to a better destiny. "O Lord . . . to thee shall the nations come, from the ends of the earth. . . ." He "who scattered" will gather and keep his people "as a shepherd keeps his flock."

4.
The Beaten and the Brave

Thick double walls surrounded ancient Babylon, its gleaming towers rearing astride the Euphrates river. From the Ishtar gate, the broad Avenue of Processions ran through the city's lavish center, flanked by statuary, palatial courts and temples to Tiamat and Marduk. There, in the midst of fashionable idolatry, imposing wealth, proud sciences, uninhibited pleasures and luxuries, the ragged, captive people of God dwelt for half a century in servitude, longing for a lost dream.

"By the waters of Babylon, there we sat down and wept," go the dirge-like verses of Psalm 137, telling of the despondency and misery of that time.

Directions blurred and purpose wavered, even to the prophets, those Jewish messengers of the divine will for humanity. Ezekiel, in his bleak vision, saw the nation turned into a valley of death, littered with broken skeletons. "Our bones are dried up, and our hope is lost." Yet out of that desolation, he and other prophets of that dark period from 587 to 538 B.C.—the dauntless Daniel and a brilliant, tender prophet whose name remains unknown — caught glimpses of a coming greater glory than ever.

81

"They who wait for the Lord shall renew their strength," wrote the poetic sage called Second Isaiah. "They shall mount up with wings like eagles, they shall run and not be weary, they shall walk and not faint ... Arise, shine, for your light has come, and the glory of the Lord has risen upon you ... and nations shall come to your light, and kings to the brightness of your rising."

The bold, perceptive Daniel, who was singled out for special duty in the retinue of the conquering Babylonian monarch, Nebuchadnezzar, also saw in a dream the tracery of an amazingly majestic future. "Behold, with the clouds of heaven, there came one like a son of man, and he came to the Ancient of Days ... And to him was given dominion and glory and kingdom, that all peoples, nations and languages should serve him; his dominion is an everlasting dominion which shall not pass away."

It was a strangely nebulous, yet beckoning image, rising from the hidden subconscious in a day of abject suffering and defeat, yet whispering of some special theophany. "A bruised reed he will not break and a dimly burning wick he will not quench ... till he has established justice in the earth," wrote the anonymous one, also called Deutero-Isaiah. "The Lord has lain on him the iniquity of us all."

This, too, was an odd, puzzling conception, yet applicable to Jesus, and it was in keeping with the shadowy, figurative symbolism in which the prophets often spoke in that melancholy period of captivity.

Under the heel of a powerful, skilled, heathen empire, Judaism's great commission of bringing knowledge of one universal God to the world seemed shattered and dead. "Shall these bones live?" came the question in Ezekiel's grim vision of a death-strewn canyon, its floor covered with skeletons. But "behold, a rattling: and the bones came together, bone to bone. And as I looked, there were sinews on them, and flesh."

And he sensed the assurance of the Almighty. "Behold, I will raise you from your graves, O my people; and I will bring you home. . . . I will put my Spirit within you, and you shall live. . . . And you shall know that I am the Lord."

Curious, visionary, born of ruin and affliction, the imagery carried a burning hope and unrelinquished conviction, smouldering beneath the lusty, bumptious and extravagant panoply of pagan Babylon.

Engineering technology, astronomy, mathematics, artworks, and cuneiform literature flourished in the academies of the affluent capital of Chaldea, along with grand-scale prostitution, addiction to drugs and drink, tyranny and altars to 2,500 gods. The gold-veneered temple of Marduk, god of the ruling order and the dominant figure of imperial devotions, towered massively beside the processional street, outrivaling shrines to Tiamat, god of chaos, and Ishtar, goddess of sensual delights. On that same dazzling street stood the resplendent palace of Nebuchadnezzar with its charming hanging gardens, richly enameled halls, suites and chambers for concubines. The whole city, haughty, artful, sated with spoils of conquest, came to be regarded as the archetype of human corruption and defiance of God— the great beast, harlot Babylon.

Nebuchadnezzar, on finding some highly learned men among his prisoners, shrewdly installed some of them in his court, assigning extensive functions to Daniel. Three others, Shadrach, Meshach, and Abednego, initially drew the king's rage and were cast into a fiery furnace for refusing to worship the royal idols of gold. But mysteriously they survived unscathed.

Daniel pointedly warned Nebuchadnezzar that his kingdom and succeeding oppressive empires were fated for destruction but that "the God of heaven will set up a kingdom which will never be destroyed." He told the king that the proud monarch himself would go mad, running wild in the fields, until he acknowledged that the one Sovereign rules humanity. The madness came, and the clarity, before Nebuchadnezzar died in 561.

Although Daniel continued in his post under the new ruler, Belshazzar, he soon came under condemnation for defying an edict not to pray to "any god or man" except to the king. Cast into a den of lions, Daniel emerged unhurt.

Unlike other writings of the prophets, the Book of Daniel relating these extraordinary events remained unknown, purportedly "shut up and sealed" until centuries later in 168 B.C., raising questions about his role and the time of the book's composition. But it specifically concerns the years of exile, including Daniel's interpretation of those mysterious words, MENE, MENE, TEKEL and PARSIN, which appeared on the wall at a rowdy feast of the new king, Belshazzar. "God has numbered the days of your kingdom. . . . You have been weighed in the balances and found wanting. . . ." That night, Belshazzar was slain.

Unlike Daniel, most of the captive Jewish population eked out a bare existence as farm laborers, servants, street sweepers, peddlers, wood carriers, and building crews, living in drab hovels with meager diets. Overseers mocked them, the Psalms relate, hooting, "Sing to us one your songs of Zion!" But the throats of the toiling captives were dry and mute and their lyres hung stringless on the willow branches. "How shall we sing the Lord's song in a foreign land?"

Despite the bitter resignation, however, that far-seeing prophet whose writings form the latter part of the book named for the earlier Isaiah (chapters 40 through 55) offered hopeful consolation.

"Comfort, comfort my people, says your God," he said. "Speak tenderly to Jerusalem . . . that her warfare is ended, that her iniquity is pardoned. . . . A voice cries in the wilderness, prepare the way of the Lord. . . . Every valley shall be lifted up, and every mountain and hill be made low. . . . And the glory of the Lord shall be revealed, and all flesh shall see it together." Again, these veiled, tenuous inklings would be applied more than 500 years later to Jesus.

Ezekiel, whose book swarms with mystical, elaborate imagery, lived in a shack beside the Chebar canal where other Jewish refugees often came for counsel. His wife died there. A solemn man, he belonged to a historic priestly family. "Our transgressions and our sins are upon us, and we waste away because of them," he mourned. "How then shall we live?" And he urged, "Repent."

He despised the Babylonians' "abominable images and their detestable things," the king's bowing before royal teraphim and inspecting the lines in a sheep's liver for revelations, the younger Jews turning to alien diversions and superstitions. Ezekiel, whose call to prophecy had come in a furious, lightning-laced thunderstorm, visualized God's appeal to humanity as pervading all the world, not just Judaism. He pictured that totality as "wheels within a wheel" moving everywhere. He also perceived man's individual free will, allowing for discord or harmony with the universal God.

Subject at times to silent, motionless trances, Ezekiel envisioned a broad life-giving river rising out of Judaism. To him it offered high hope ahead.

Daniel remained a regal adjutant through Babylonia's collapse in 539. Under the expanding new Persian empire and into the rule of its more benevolent King Cyrus, he conceived of an approaching "everlasting kingdom" over all the earth.

Generally, the messianic hopes and yearnings looked toward some divinely exalted and blissful world sovereignty, but Second Isaiah added a shocking note to that concept, saying: "He had no form or comeliness that we should look at him, and no beauty that we should desire him. He was despised and rejected by men; a man of sorrows, acquainted with grief. . . .

Surely he has borne our griefs. . . . Yet we esteemed him stricken, smitten by God, and afflicted. But he was wounded for our transgressions, he was bruised for our iniquities; upon him was the chastisement that made us whole, and with his stripes we are healed. . . . Yet it was the will of the Lord to bruise him. . . . When he makes himself an offering for our sin, he shall see his offspring, he shall prolong his days; the will of the Lord shall prosper his hand; he shall see the fruit of the travail of his soul and be satisfied; by his knowledge shall the righteous one, my servant, make many to be accounted righteous, and he shall bear their iniquities."

Those strange, anticipatory insights, along with others, are known as the "suffering servant" passages, which many Christians see as portraying the persecution and death of Jesus in union with humanity and in recompense for its evildoing.

Cyrus, the new master of the middle east, released the exiles in 538 B.C. to go home, and Second Isaiah foresaw that joyous time approaching. He offered cheering encouragement, suffused with those happy, peculiar intimations of a world-sweeping redemption.

Jubilant, confident, brimming with a sense of new purpose and soaring expectancy in the waning hours of a long night of soul-searching, Second Isaiah also used words that Jesus himself would quote as his text in his first sermon five centuries later in Nazareth:

"The Spirit of the Lord God is upon me, because the Lord has anointed me to bring good tidings to the afflicted; he has sent me to bind up the brokenhearted, to proclaim liberty to the captives, and the opening of the prisons to those who are bound; to proclaim the year of the Lord's favor."

5.
The Late Watchmen

As in all times, the people waiting for the dawn of an idyllic realm found that it didn't come easily or all at once. It wasn't prefabricated. It wasn't superimposed. They themselves were involved. Instead of perfect felicity, they met the whirlwind.

It had human features. It bore their nature. They teneted the world and they encountered their kind. They confronted man's reality. And it swept on them in recurring gusts, like the swift, passing flurries before the gale, like the intermittent rumbles before the mountain falls.

Out of their insufficiency, they pleaded, "Come thou longed-for One."

It was a far-spread prayer of those tumultuous centuries preceding the birth of Jesus, murmuring beyond the borders of monotheistic Judaism, rustling in the pantheons of the clashing empires of Egypt, Persia, Syria, Greece, and finally Rome. The golden dream plucked at mankind's heart.

But it was an amorphous, varied aspiration, often reckoned as the rise of some peerless nationalistic dominion or else the great eschaton itself—the end of time and opening of eternity.

"Behold, a man riding upon a red horse!" "I see a flying scroll." "Behold, a man with a measuring line in his hand." The symbolic impressions tumbled from the prophet Zechariah about 520 B.C., alluding to a hoped-for messiah. "Sing and rejoice, O daughters of Zion, for lo, I come, and I will dwell in the midst of you, says the Lord."

Another contemporary Jerusalem prophet, Haggai, wrote: "I am about to shake the heavens and earth, says the Lord, I will shake all nations so that the treasures of all nations come in, and I will fill this house with splendor." But Haggai sorely miscalculated the identity of the "chosen one," singling out a soon banished princeling, Zerubbabel.

So disappointments and troubles came — barely home from Babylonian captivity, they were pitted against doubt, poverty, plagues of locusts, false leaders, invasions, alien despotism, and civil war. Then came the abomination of abominations—the installing in the Temple Holy of Holies an altar to a pagan idol, the mythological Greek god Zeus.

Revolution, guerrilla warfare and massive reprisals stalked the land. "No ruler but God" became the underground battle-cry. Outbursts of the conflict still would remain in Jesus' day, sending his immediate forerunner, John the Baptist, to the chopping block.

Back from their long exile, the people found a waste-land. Jerusalem was a fire-blackened rubble and heathen tribes wandered about the ravished province. Depressed and disheartened, the returning Jews sought to rebuild their country. But drought parched the fields, withered the vines and left their oil jars unfilled. Spirits sagged and efforts slackened. "You have sown much and harvested little," said Haggai. "You have looked for much, and lo, it came to little."

A pragmatic prophet, he roused them to get back

to work to build the Lord's Temple as a prelude to divine kingship and plenitude. "Take courage, all you people of the land, says the Lord: work, for I am with you."

Zechariah also urged them on, and once again, cedar logs were floated from Lebanon to Joppa, brought overland by camels to Jerusalem. Carpentry and masonry hummed in Jerusalem and the towns of Israel. Zechariah, in a burst of exultation, offered a bright forecast:

"Rejoice greatly, O daughter of Zion! Lo, your king comes to you; triumphant and victorious is he, humble and riding on an ass, on a colt the foal of an ass . . . and he shall command peace to the nations; his dominion shall be from sea to sea, and from the river to the ends of the earth."

But Zechariah also emphasized humanity's part in building that new tomorrow. "Render true judgments, show kindness and mercy . . . do not oppress the widow, the fatherless, the sojourner or the poor. . . . Speak the truth and make for peace." And he observed, "Not by might, nor by power, but by my Spirit, says the Lord."

Judea, as the province came to be called, now was controlled by the Persian empire under Darius I. It held sway until 332 B.C.—for 200 years. Early in that period, Persia's marauding armies crossed the area looting, en route to conquer Egypt.

Other roving bands harassed the struggling Jewish state in its rehabilitation efforts, sometimes forcing laborers to keep a sword at hand and infesting the country with cults of Ishtar, Tammuz, the sun and moon.

But the prophet Zechariah gave encouragement. "Sing", counseled the figure of his vision whose hand held a measuring line, "for lo, I come and I will dwell in the midst of you, says the Lord. And many nations shall join themselves to the Lord in that day, and shall be my people."

As Zechariah saw it, the prospect also had to do with government, better economics, and plentiful rain for the crops. "For there shall be a sowing of peace and prosperity; the vine shall yield its fruit, and the ground shall give its increase. And the Lord will become king over all the earth."

Yet Zechariah also had brooding premonitions about it, of a coming "shepherd of the flock," carrying a staff named "Grace" in one hand and "Union" in the other, but whose staffs would be broken and who would be sold out for thirty pieces of silver.

The Jewish Temple, which spurred the legacy of the prophets on which Christianity has its base, was finally restored in 516 B.C. The ensuing prophet, Malachi, worked to rectify worship, to reinforce religious disciplines and ethical standards. But in the face of hardships came apathy, disillusionment and skepticism, along with infiltrations of heathen religions, pagan intermarriage, adultery, perjury, victimizing of the poor, a disinterested priesthood.

But Malachi insisted on revitalizing hope ahead. "They shall be mine, says the Lord of hosts . . . on the day when I act, and I will spare them as a man spares his son who serves him. The sun of righteousness shall rise, with its healing wings. You shall go forth leaping like calves from the stall . . .

"Behold, I send my messenger to prepare the way before me, and the Lord whom you seek will suddenly come to his Temple; the messenger of the covenant in whom you delight, he is coming. Behold, I will send you Elijah the prophet before the great and terrible day of the Lord comes."

In the later time of John the Baptist, the desert herald of Jesus was considered Elijah returned.

But despite the heady anticipations, no quick, automatic paradise came. The adversities continued, including a sky-blackening plague of locusts, stripping orchards, pastures and fields, swarming on windows, pouring into houses, wreaking havoc on the country. Whether allegorical or real, naturalists say the graphic descriptions by the prophet Joel in about 400 B.C. of the devastating onslaught of locusts accurately portrays their ferocity.

To Joel, it was like a forest fire and the very earth seemed to shudder. He saw it as a sign of God's manifestation, to call men to stark account for their oppression, plunder, deceit, mutual abuse and violence, the consequences to reach their climax in the valley of judgment—Jehoshaphat.

But even in Joel's apocalytic interpretation of historic time being brought to its consummation, he saw a bright promise for God's people. "Fear not, O land; be glad . . . you will be satisfied. A fountain shall come forth from the house of the Lord." Joel also used words that Peter later would quote at Pentecost at the outpouring of God's spirit as promised by Jesus on the myriad races of humanity.

"And it shall come to pass afterward, that I will pour out my spirit on all flesh; your sons and your daughters shall prophesy, your old men shall dream dreams, and your young men shall see visions."

Persian domination collapsed in 333 B.C. before the world-conquering armies of Alexander the Great, a student of Aristotle, spreading Hellenistic influences into the holy city of Jerusalem, including public baths, gymnasiums, theaters, and the galaxy of Greek gods. At Alexander's early death, the Greek empire was divided between his generals, Seleucus in Syria and Ptolemy I over Egypt. Judea, like a lamb between two lions, was under Egypt's control from 312 to 198 B.C., when the Syrian Seleucid empire seized it after defeating the Egyptians.

In 168, the hated Syrian overlord Antiochus, who called himself Epiphanes, meaning "God manifest," acted to stamp out Judaism's dedication to one universal God. He outlawed Jewish worship and commanded devotions to the Greek gods of Zeus, Ares and Aphrodite. His militia plundered the Temple, murdered priests, burned religious scrolls, carried off the golden-branched candlesticks and rich scarlet draperies, razed the Temple outbuildings and apartments. In the inner Temple court, he set up the figure of Zeus and ordered all Judean villages to erect similar shrines and pay homage to them.

In the northern hamlet of Modin, an old priest, Mattathias Maccabaeus, refused an order to make offerings to a Greek idol, slew the guard commanding him to do so, smashed the heathen altar and with his five sons fled to the hills.

That spark — in 166 — ignited revolution. A son, Judas Maccabaeus, "the Hammerer," gathered a guerrilla band. Hiding, striking suddenly, withdrawing, striking by surprise again, the tactics gradually wore down the mighty legions of Syria and in two years drove them from the land.

Judea, as of old, was again its own. Little Judea, which over the centuries had been periodically invaded, sacked, occupied, enslaved and ruled by successive empires of Assyria, Egypt, Babylonia, Greece and Syria, at last was free of the foreign yoke.

The cleansing of the defiled Temple and its rededication to God in 164 B.C. is celebrated annually by Judaism about the same time that Christians celebrate the birth of Jesus. The happy holiday, Hanukkah, the "Festival of Lights," commemorates the way in which Temple lamps at its restoration had burned for eight days although there was only enough oil on hand for one day.

For a century, Judean independence was maintained, but only against constant harassment by Syria which regained control for a brief ten-year interlude and lost it again, leaving the country in turmoil. There was factional conflict and intermittent civil war, with the rising power-minded Sadducean party gaining control of the priesthood and executing thousands of devout Pharisees who sought to preserve religious vitality and learning.

Although prophecy had lapsed for four centuries, the dream of a messiah grew stronger. In 63 B.C., Rome's conquering legions under Pompey seized Jerusalem and Rome became the new master of Judea, remaining in control until the state was wiped out in 70 A.D., not to rise again until modern times.

Herod the Great, a crafty, cruel man, was installed by Rome on the provincial throne, and 33 years later, on hearing reports of a "King" born in Bethlehem, he sent troops to slay all male children under two.

But the massacre missed its prey. A new scepter was quietly rising among the people, and in time, a new, rugged prophet came striding out of the wilderness, clad in camel-hair cloak and leather belt, proclaiming an excited message on the banks of the Jordan River.

"Prepare the way of the Lord!" declared John the Baptist. "He who is mightier than I is coming, the throng of whose sandals I am not worthy to untie."

Many listened. The words rang strong and a worried government had the prophet silenced and finally executed. Sorrowing over it, Jesus later would look out over the city that symbolized mankind's finest ideals and greatest hope, saying: "O Jerusalem, Jerusalem, killing the prophets and stoning those who are sent to you."

PART 3
Glimpses of the Galilean

1.
A Father's Imprint

Straining hard, Joseph hoisted the huge beam above his head and lowered it into the notched pillars. He was a muscular, toil-toughened man with gnarled, gristly hands and a back of iron. He was a *naggar,* as his native Aramaic tongue called it, a builder and worker in wood. Out of his sweat, skill, and care he set the model of manhood for Jesus, the young son who labored with him.

Although rarely noted, this was the powerful influence from which Jesus drew his singularly trusting and intimate imagery of God as "Father"—a nuance and phrasing previously unheard of in the Judaism of that day in referring to the Almighty. For Jesus, that father figure and its connotations of great strength, dependability, and unwavering personal affection derived from the one who filled that earthly responsibility for him. The one who reared him from boyhood, the carpenter and joiner of Nazareth, Joseph.

He left a deep imprint. In the culture of that time, the father held unchallenged sway over his household, a patriarch whose authority was unquestionable and who was responsible for guiding his family. "Train up a child in the way he should go, and when he is old he will not depart from it," Scripture counseled Jewish fathers. And Joseph held firmly to that belief.

He was a poor, rugged, but resourceful man; a woodchip behind his ear as a sign of his trade, a scarred leather apron tied across his waist. Beside him worked the young Jesus, an apprentice in the craft, subject to him. "Just as it is necessary to feed one's son, so it is necessary to teach him a manual trade," the rabbis taught, and Joseph followed that tradition with Jesus.

In the customs of that period, a male son remained in the mother's care until the age of five, when the father took over the child's training, both religiously and vocationally. The "carpenter's son," the villagers called Jesus. The older man and youngster became steady partners, in toil and private talk. Theirs was a long, close-knit comradeship, fashioned by the force of common necessity to labor for provisioning their table.

Joseph, after lifting the wall joist into place, boosted the boy of twelve athwart it to nail it fast, instructing him on how to slant the iron spikes. The heavy joists would support rafters to hold up a roof of clay. "Unless the Lord builds the house, those who build it labor in vain," went an old maxim of Joseph's heritage. But "an artisan in his work need not defer to the greatest of doctors. Whatever your work, commit it to the Lord, and your plan will be established."

Throughout the years of Jesus' youth, he spent most of his waking hours with Joseph, learning to manage wood, to choose materials, to calculate sizes and shapes, to mitre a joint, to dowel a table, to taper a wheelspoke to a hub.

The pair often went into the forests of sycamore, cypress, and firs to fetch raw timber. Joseph taught the youth to wield an axe, to cut low to avoid stump waste, how to govern the tree fall so it would drop in a clearing and not damage other trees. Together they would carry the big logs back to Joseph's workshed to saw them into slabs, dress and work them into carts, chests, doors, buckets, yokes, and wooden plowshares.

"Father, how is this frame braced?" the questions and directions would flow to and fro as they worked, the sawdust and shavings piling up beneath their bare feet. "Hand me an awl." "Here, turn the crank while I hold the drill." The callous hands often were bruised and nicked from blade or hammer.

A father's tutelage also instilled the son with the history and teachings of Judaism, its special mandate as lightbearer to the world, its law and prophets as commanded in Scripture:

"These words . . . shall be upon your heart; and you shall teach them diligently to your children, and shall talk of them when you sit in your house, and when you walk by the way, and when you lie down, and when you rise."

The nub of these precepts, from which Jesus would often quote later, was in the great Shema, a prayer of commitment spoken morning and night and contained in a small box of parchment attached to the doorpost of each Jewish home. "Hear, O Israel: The Lord our God is one Lord," the words read. "And you shall love the Lord your God with all your heart and with all your soul and with all your mind." Each day as Joseph and Jesus left the house in Nazareth, they would touch the mezuza containing that vow and then put their fingers to their lips.

Similar texts were inscribed in small cases on leather bands, the phylacteries, which they wore tied about their heads and to their left hands at Sabbath worship when Jesus and Joseph sat together in fringed coats. Mary sat in a separate women's section.

Occasionally, after the lifting of the scroll of Scripture from the ark and bell-ringing procession with it, Joseph would be summoned to the central desk, the tebah, to read the day's lesson, while an admiring Jesus sat listening. As a youth, Jesus also doubtlessly attended the synagogue school, the *Bet Hakeneset,* sitting cross-legged on a floor mat with other boys in a bare, rectangular room decorated only with the Star of David and the seven-branched menorah. The chazzan taught from a front bench.

Ancient accounts tell of Jesus' childhood, problems, and play, of his molding clay birds by a brook, confounding teachers and Joseph's defense of him, of his being falsely accused of pushing a playmate, Zeno, off a roof, of his breaking a water pitcher and once getting his ear wrung by Joseph. But the two showed constant devotion to each other.

Their household hummed day-long with benedictions. Every action brought forth a blessing of God for it: on awakening, dressing, on tying a sandal, at meals, for work, for thunder and sun, on going to bed. All existence was acclaimed sacred. "Blessed art thou, O Lord, our God, King of the universe who hast made thy world ... who hast produced goodly creatures ... who createst fragrant woods ... who givest good ... who bestowest loving kindness ... who hast made firm the steps of man."

2.
A Lost Son

When the search first began, Joseph had not been overly concerned. The boy no doubt was with other young men somewhere in the caravan. But gradually, finding no sign or word of him, the level-headed Joseph felt the small, beginning edge of alarm.

Jesus apparently was missing. Either he had abandoned his family and tribe, run away, or else had become lost in the teeming city. Any parent who has ever experienced the disappearance of a child knows the pangs of it—the gathering shock and helplessness and loss. Joseph ranged back and forth through the home-bound procession of Passover pilgrims, a sinking emptiness in him, his voice hoarse from calling, "Yeshua! Yeshua!" Finally, the entire company of Galilean kinspeople and acquaintances halted on the road while a thorough search was made.

The lad was not there. Other youngsters were questioned. None had seen Jesus all day. Women began murmuring sympathetically, "Haval, haval . . . woe, woe!" Mary became tearful, her chin quivering. Joseph took her firmly by the shoulders. They would find the boy, he said. Do not fear. They must return to Jerusalem.

Already, the band had traveled a full day's journey en route to rural Galilee after the festival week in the capital of Israel. But Joseph and Mary, in their worried haste, retraced the distance in about half the time. It had been the first "going up to Jerusalem" in which

Joseph had permitted Jesus to come along, initiating him into the religious duties.

Scripture instructed Jewish males to present themselves thrice annually at the Temple in Jerusalem on each of the three solemn celebrations, or at least once annually if residing far away. Women were not obligated to make the trips but could do so, as Mary did, if their husbands wished it.

At the age of twelve, the boy approach many duties as a "son of the Torah," and Joseph had considered the time ripe to allow him to make his initial pilgrimage to the holy city. But now, given that privilege, he had used it to stray off somewhere, telling no one, and without parental consent. He had always been a considerate, obedient son, yet with a strikingly original turn of mind. Hurrying, without pausing to rest, Joseph and Mary climbed back up the steep road that ascended from the lowland of Jericho and the Dead Sea into the desolate Judean hills. Reaching the plateau town of Bethany, they again could see the spires and turrets of Jerusalem.

It was a mixed, multifarious place now. The foreign dominion of Rome and its collaborators, infected with sundry snares and pitfalls would endanger a young peasant boy alone, especially among the motley thousands that jammed the city for the holidays. The alien rulers had introduced pagan games and entertainments, the battling at the hippodrome among gladiators and of condemned prisoners and slaves with beasts, a theater of magicians, acrobats and wispily clad dancers.

Roman soldiers, barechested wrestlers, painted and bespangled harlots, pipers to snakes, sellers of elixirs and intoxicating potions, false dealers, thieves, and soothsayers swarmed the streets. There were Assyrians, Egyptians, Greeks, and Babylonians, with their impure, non-Kosher foods and wanton rites to idols of Bacchus and Astarte.

Joseph and Mary descended into the valley of

Jehoshaphat outside the city's eastern wall, crossed the brook of Kidron and started their hunt in the sprawling camp where they had stayed during Passover, a tent city of the poor outside the city of stone. They threaded through the far-spread maze of goathair shelters, smoking campfires, garbage heaps, clouds of flies, hanging bedding, improvised shops, and loitering clusters of people. They continued on, asking questions, scrutinizing each group of romping children, but finding no trace of Jesus.

Darkness came on. After being inspected for arms at the Siloam gate by Roman soldiers, the couple entered the lower city and began tramping its narrow streets, weaving through its milling bazaars and markets, peering into dim alleys and gaming rooms.

They took no rest that night and got little of it in the harried days that followed. Occasionally they dozed briefly and fitfully beside a wall or roofed pool where others of the poor, the sackcloth-clad mendicants, and the lame were allowed respite. Through the winding passages and plazas of the city they stalked, tired-eyed and forlorn, along the streets of the cheese-mongers, the bakers, the metalsmiths, up the steps into the western upper city with is grand houses, arcades, fountains, and the palace of Herod; back down into the dusty Acra with its clogged, babbling marketplace, its hawkers of tonics, fabrics and neck-banded slaves.

For three days, they searched back and forth, up one twisting byway and down another until the scenes blurred and became a bewildering jumble. They searched on, inquiring, appealing to watchmen and gatekeepers, dulled to the brusque rejoinders, riven with nameless fears of unnumbered dire possibilities.

Several times, they had hunted through the Temple, its courts, colonnades, and tunnels beneath it, circling the adjacent Tower of Antonia from which the Roman garrison kept watch, but all in vain. Finally, they again plodded up the sloping pavement to the Temple and into its rectilinear succession of courts. Sidling among its crowds and commerce, their eyes glazed from looking, they moved past the tables of moneychangers and pens of bleating lambs and flapping pigeons, on into the inner courts of horn-shaped collection boxes, the Levite musicians on the semi-circular stairs, the priests sending up smoke and incense from the great altar.

Exhausted, despairing, strained to the breaking point, the pair wandered at length out onto one of the colonnaded porches where groups of learned doctors and scholars of theology and law taught their students and engaged in analytical discussions. Joseph, his big shoulders slumping, stared at them leadenly. Then a sound caught his ears. It was a boy's voice, serious, animated, probing. Jesus! Joseph touched Mary's shoulder and she heard it, too, her face flooding with unutterable relief. Then she rushed across the floor, pressing through the circle of scholars, oblivious to their shushing, and confronted the boy.

"Son, why have you treated us so?" she demanded. "Behold, your father and I have been looking for you anxiously." It was a mother's natural burst of pent-up distress after the long, heart-rending days of futile search and mounting desperation. Jesus looked up at her with innocent appeal, concerned by her reprimand, yet seeming curiously convinced he had been doing the right and appropriate thing. "How is it that you sought me?" he said. "Did you not know that I must be in my Father's house?" They stood there, his mother's eyes filling, and then their arms flew around one another.

Joseph, drawing a long breath of sheer gratitude, dropped down on a knee beside them, hugging them both, feeling Jesus' ardently devoted kiss through his uncombed beard. Thanks be to God! The boy was all right, whatever his deflecting fascination with these religious sages. Joseph lifted him up in his arms, giving hm a hearty, thankful squeeze. "My son, my son!" He was safe and well, thank God, safe and well.

Scripture notes that neither he nor Mary understood what the boy meant by his insistence that he had some justifiably overriding interest here in the center of Israel's faith, exceeding duties to his immediate family. They also had been puzzled by the scholars' absorption in him, their attentiveness to his inquiries and penetrating comments.

Apparently he had been with them throughout the time of his absence. Jesus, a country boy of twelve so engrossed with his first personal encounter with the hallowed city, its disparate life, the Temple's imposing ceremonies of worship and sacrifice, the issues troubling the great religious academies, that he had to drink it all in, to find out its ways and assess it in his own way. Regardless of the family he loved, he had been compelled to do it out of a sense of some further calling and wider love.

Joseph didn't grasp all this and probably wasn't occupied on that level at the time. What mattered was that after a prolonged, tormenting nightmare about the welfare of a lost son, the boy was back now, unharmed and sound, as fine as ever. They returned to Nazareth and Jesus remained obedient to them, increasing in wisdom and stature, a credit to a pleased Joseph. It was something to be glad about, and proud of. The carpenter had a good son.

At thirten, on the first Sabbath of his fourteenth year, Jesus reached the time for his bar mitzvah, his coming of age as a "son of the Torah," a man of duty, taking up adult religious responsibilities. "I summon to the honor of the Torah our young brother, ha-gadol Yeshua," said the presiding elder after unrolling the scroll on the tebah. "Let the young man come up! May the Lord strengthen, bless, and keep him."

It was the first occasion for Jesus to don the tallith (prayer shawl), lead the congregational prayers, and read the day's Scripture passages. It has been speculated that he read from the prophet Zechariah including these phrases: "Sing and rejoice, O daughter of Zion; for lo, I come and I will dwell in the midst of you, says the Lord. And many nations shall join themselves to me in that day, and shall be my people . . . Not by might, nor by power, but by my Spirit, says the Lord of hosts."

Afterward came the well-wishing of neighbors and proud parents. Jesus had entered maturity but he remained for years in close association with Joseph, becoming known as a carpenter himself before he began his ministry at the age of thirty.

Together, their toolsacks slung over their shoulders, the two men kept to the rhythms of the rustic life around them, delivering finished items at houses in Nazareth, repairing gates, threshing boards, and presses on nearby farms. They watched women grinding corn, sewing, measuring meal, leavening dough, activities familiar in Jesus' later illustrations. They mingled with farmers sowing grain, digging out tares in the wheat, hunting a lost sheep. They gazed at lilies of the field, circling eagle, a fox's hole and bird's nest, chatted with children, all of these subsequently flavoring Jesus' teaching.

Sometime before Jesus' ministry began, Joseph died. The old accounts describe him as becoming weak, cold, and stiff. Jesus helped him lie down on a mat of straw and sat cradling his head, stroking his brow, as Joseph uttered his final words, "Oh my child, my Jesus."

Although Jesus was born of Mary, it was Joseph who shaped the man. It was Joseph who found shelter at his birth on that first Christmas, who shielded him from danger, who earned his bread, who trained him in work, nurtured him in faith. It was Joseph who reared the one regarded by generations since as manifesting the ways of God to humanity. And to do that, Jesus turned to a tender, personal name whose meaning rang so strong in him—"Father."

3.
The Workman

In a steady rhythm, the axe rose and fell, biting into the base of the tall sycamore. Every two strokes, one swinging sideways and the next slicing downward, sent a fat chip flying. He rarely missed. It was an instinctive skill, born, shaped, and seasoned into him by upbringing and years of toil.

Breathing hard, Jesus stepped aside as the tree swayed with a slow, cracking groan, as if in a final desperate protest against the gash tearing at its heart, and then it fell with a roar and lay silent. The sun rode low, past the eighth hour. He trimmed off the limbs and lifted one end of the log, levering it up on his bare back until he got it balanced across his shoulders behind his head, and then he started home.

It was good timber, cut after the autumn's last growth when the sap was down. A craftsman respected his materials. That was far more than the oppressors of Israel did for its people, even when they were pliantly submissive. "If they do this when the wood is green," he would later observe, "what will happen when it is dry?" When revolt did come, Caesar would crush it with massive destruction. Already many had died, and thousands of Jews, including children, had been shipped to Rome as slaves.

Tradition says that for about twenty years, from the time Jesus became a "son of the Torah" at thirteen, until he was thirty-three, he had worked at his trade. After Joseph's death Jesus took over the support of the family, including his mother Mary, and it was hard but worthy labor. They were of "low estate," as she once described it, poor but devoutly responsible.

Under pressures of making ends meet, he watched against waste. In later days, Scripture notes that he twice had his men gather up scraps of food "that nothing may be lost." He was a saver, in the deepest sense. He was familiar with patched clothes, pointing out that the patch ought to be shrunk like the garment or it would rip loose. He also understood the necessity of having to borrow bread from a friend's house to feed an unexpected hungry guest, even though the hour was late and it troubled the friend to have to dress and come down to unbar the gate.

Nevertheless, "Ask, and it will be given you," Jesus advised. "Seek, and you will find; knock, and it will be opened unto you."

From the valley, sinking now in shadows, it was a long, hard climb up the mountainside to Nazareth. He struggled along under the weight of the tree trunk, its bark digging pits across his sinewy back, gnats swarming about his face. Sometimes, no doubt, he snaked the logs up the mountain by burro, or hired cutters for it. In subsequent remarks, he showed keen familiarity with an employer's duty to laborers, and of the forethought essential to construction contracts.

"For which of you, desiring to build a tower, does not first sit down and count the cost . . . ? Otherwise, when he has laid the foundation and is unable to finish, all who see it begin to mock him, saying, "This man began to build and was not able to finish.'"

He also maintained, in a parable regarded as depicting his own great-hearted ultimate role, that a householder had a right to pay his men more than they earned, to fill needs of the scantily employed as much as the fulltime jobholders. "Do you begrudge my generosity? . . . The last will be first, and the first last."

The woodworking shop in Nazareth must have included the usual tools of that region and period—wedges, knives, awls, drillbits worked with a bow string, measuring rods, plummets, set-squares, bronze nails, and the multipurposed adze. Here the raw timber was split, planed into boards and made into tables, threshing floors, and cabinets; or carved into wheels, yokes, and ploughs — farm items for which Jesus was especially noted, according to ancient legend.

It was strenuous labor of the deft hand and accurate eye, of sweat, straining muscles and aching fatigue, of callous palms, throbbing bruises and the sweet sleep which only heavy exertions can bring. Jesus turned out dependable workmanship; he was highly regarded, increasing in "favor with God and man." Such a reputation among fellow townsmen indicates he was a fair dealer, reliable in filling orders, considerate in his charges, prompt in paying for supplies.

On business in the marketplace, the identifying mark of his trade was a woodchip stuck behind an ear; dyers wore a colored cloth, weavers a large bone needle thrust in front of their tunics. Scribes carried a pen.

Besides handcrafting items, woodworkers also built houses, erecting frames, securing limestone and basalt from quarriers for walls, laying rooftrees to hold up the reed wattling packed with clay to form flat rooftops. Out of practiced experience, Jesus could speak later of the foolhardiness of building a house on sand, where it would collapse from flood and winds, instead of on rock, where it would withstand the elements.

Although generally esteemed, he had a singularly independent turn of mind, calling him beyond his own clan and livelihood. It was a mission which he asserted he could not do on his own authority, regardless of how wise or able. "I seek not my own will but the will of him who sent me."

Distractions tugged at him, coaxing him to use his capacities for personal aggrandizement. He was tempted, Scripture says, an affectionate, proficient, vital man, found of children and home life, tempted to push his own interests, yet forgoing it to give himself to others. "This is my beloved Son in whom I am well pleased," came the divine confirmation to the carpenter who carried the heavy trees up the mountainside and who said, "My yoke is easy, and my burden is light."

To ease that burden for others, at the anguished pith of existence, was the dominant chord within him; to bring rest to "all who labor and are heavy-laden"— even though it would mean shouldering a rougher tree —the cross. Yet the woodworker always loved wood, the smell of it, the touch, the scaffolding it gave to the human habitat. Heaven itself, as he once described it, was like a tree nourished in the good earth, like a tiny seed springing up until it became a great sheltering monarch, a homing place for all the creatures of the air—one that would never fall to a man's axe.

And at the last, the crack carpenter of Nazareth, the man of the hard arms, the quick hands, and sure eye, said he still had a construction project to work on. "I go to prepare a place for you." It would be a "house of many rooms," firmly anchored, well proportioned, built by a professional.

4.
A Cooperating Cousin

A prisonkeeper twisted an eight-inch key in the lock and pulled open the heavy, creaking door. He went down twenty stone steps into the black rockhewn dungeon, kicked the prisoner to his feet and brought him out in chains. The thin, shaggy man, clad in a camel pelt, blinked unseeingly into the daylight. He was a cousin of Jesus.

Guards led him to a wooden block and shoved him to his knees, clamping his neck down into the stocks. One of the soldiers raised a long broadsword in both hands and brought it swishing down, cutting off the head of John the Baptizer. "He was a burning and shining lamp," Jesus said of him.

The two were of the same age. They shared in the same movement. John prepared the ground for it, and in its beginning stage, came to his violent end under orders of King Herod Antipas of Galilee. Herod "feared lest the great influence John had over the people might put it in his power or inclination to raise a rebellion," writes Josephus. But the execution did not calm the king's fears nor did it stay the work started by that pair of contrasting but complementary kinsmen, John and Jesus.

111

"He must increase, but I must decrease," John said shortly before his fateful arrest. "This joy of mine is now full." Out of this kind of tie, of blood, loyalty and conviction, grew the world-spanning brotherhood which they commenced. It was not an individualistic, separately sacred enterprise. It was merged in the human stream. It was generated among men, in their race, their realm. It had an ancestry and a heritage. Its descendants are "fellow heirs," wrote St. Paul, "members of the same body."

That, in its breadth, is the family tree of Christ. "I am the vine," he said, "you are the branches." The generations of the earth, from Adam on, flowed into that lineage. It was joined with the problems of every age—hunger, hostility, violence, death. It was interknit, connected, engrained with men's flesh and faculties. It was like a seed sown in a field, Jesus said, "and the field is the . . . world."

That wider relationship was also reflected in its specific origins, in the comprehensive blood line of that child born at Bethlehem. He had a mixed host of relatives. He came of prime stock. It spawned a large intimate circle of varied attitudes in his time, in addition to the rugged ally, John.

It also went far back into the misty sources of life. In the recorded genealogy of Jesus, Matthew traces it back to Abraham, the wandering bedouin chieftain from the remote area of human origins in the Tigris-Euphrates valley. Luke's Gospel traces the line even further back to the prototype of mankind, to Adam, the son of God, whose name means the species, "humanity."

Those lists of progenitors include all sorts of people, great and lowly, noble and devious, shepherds and kings, honored monarchs such as David and Solomon and despots such as Rehoboam—a spectrum of human character. Assorted racial strains, Hittite, Moabite, Canaanite, also mingle in that Israelite line, including dependable women such as Ruth and scandal-tainted women such as Bathsheba who betrayed her husband; Tamar who tricked Judah into fathering her child, and Rahab, the harlot flax dyer of Jericho, all ancestors of Jesus.

Since both parallels and differences appear in the lists, some scholars regard Luke's record as forebearers of Jesus' mother, Mary, and Matthew's as those of her husband, Joseph, legally regarded as Jesus' father. Both Mary and Joseph were of the Davidic line, a prolific one, with numerous offspring.

One of Mary's older cousins, Elizabeth, wife of the Temple priest, Zacharias, was the mother of John the Baptist, born only six months before Jesus, It was to Elizabeth's home in the hills near Jerusalem that Mary journeyed to announce her pregnancy. "Blessed is the fruit of your womb," Elizabeth exclaimed. "For behold, the babe in my womb leaped for joy."

When John was born, his aged father exulted, "And your child will be called the prophet of the Most High."

Unlike Jesus who grew up in the close association of people and who followed the woodworking trade of Joseph, John shunned his father's priestly vocation and withdrew from society. He took to the desolate region southeast of Jerusalem toward the Dead Sea where scrolls of the ascetic Essenes have been found in caves. In solitude and silence, John steeled his character and deciphered his callings. Garbed in camel hide, he lived on dried locusts and tree honey, alone among the dunes, watching the wind trace its strange symmetries in the sand, hearing the lonely night make conversation, absorbing the cadences of eternity.

When ready, at about the age of thirty, he came storming out of the brooding wastelands, a grizzled, apocalyptic figure, burned dark by the sun, proclaiming to a restive, oppressed people, "Prepare the way of the Lord . . . all flesh shall see the salvation of God!"

"Who are you?" the anxious asked. "I am the voice of one crying in the wilderness, 'Make straight the way of the Lord . . . After me comes he who is mightier than I, the thong of whose sandals I am not worthy to stoop down and untie. I have baptized you with water, but he will baptize you with the Holy Spirit."

John had no inkling it would be his cousin, and whether the two had seen much of each other since boyhood is uncertain. At first, when Jesus offered himself for baptism, John protested his own comparative unworthiness, but Jesus insisted. "Let it be so now; for thus it is fitting for us to fulfill all righteousness." In that, too, the man of Nazareth linked himself with his fellowmen, involving himself in all humanity's need.

A dove circled and mystic tones vibrated in the air. "My beloved son. . . ." "Behold, the Lamb of God," John cried. "I myself did not know . . . but he who sent me . . . he on whom you see the Spirit descend and remain, this is he."

John continued his ministry for at least a year afterward, not only in Bethabara, but at Bethany near Jerusalem, at the village of Aenon near Salim, and in Peraea beyond the Jordan before being imprisoned. This kinsman of Jesus not only stirred such official alarm that Herod feared an uprising, but John also had assailed the king for violating Jewish moral law by divorcing his wife, to marry his brother's wife, Herodias.

It was she, Scripture relates, who advised her daughter, Salome, to ask for the imprisoned John's head. Herod, pleased with her dancing at a palace party, offered her anything she wanted. And John's "head was brought on a platter and given to the girl, and she brought it to her mother." The baptizer's disciples came and took his body, buried it and reported to Jesus what had happened. "Truly," Jesus said, "among those born of women, there has risen no one greater than John the Baptist."

The two were different in habits. John was solitary,

stern, accusatory. He fasted much, spurned strong drink. Jesus was gregarious, serene, confidently consoling, relishing a banquet. But the strictly abstemious relative left a lasting imprint. Twenty years after he was killed, the missionary Paul encountered followers of John in far-off Ephesus, including the learned Alexandrian Jew, Apollos.

And the spark John struck in Judea flamed in the ensuing ministry of Jesus, the force of it still haunting Herod. "John I beheaded, but who is this about whom I hear such rumors?" he worried. "John whom I beheaded has been raised." It wasn't that, of course; but it was a member of the same family, carrying on and finishing a job, bringing a seed to fruition.

5.
The Mixer

A rough and disreputable crew reclined around the low semi-circular table at the house in Capernaum—swagbellied vendors, sailors, fish picklers, camel drivers, crooked tax collectors, and brawling stevedores from the city wharfs. With lusty relish, they fed on broiled fresh mullet, dipping hot bread into the bowls of olive sauce and corn pottage, munching the spiced leeks and onions, washing it down with wine.

Among them, cultivating their company, was Jesus. Toward the doorway, beyond the row of hanging lamps, stood a shadowy cluster of spectators who had wandered into the open court to watch, as often occurred. They whispered among themselves, "Extortioners . . . devil's spawn."

Two of Jesus' men, themselves brawny fishermen, edged over to the group. A sternly pious scholar demanded: "Why does your teacher eat with tax collectors and sinners?" Jesus heard it, and he and the others paused in their meal. He looked about at them thoughtfully. Indeed they were a wayward lot, unstable, scorned, and they knew it, without pretense. They needed—wanted—reclaiming friendship.

Deliberatively he wiped his mouth with a towel and turned toward the chastizers beyond the smoky light. "Those who are well have no need of a physician." He quoted the prophet Hosea, " 'I desire mercy and not sacrifice,' " and added: "Go learn what this means . . . I came not to call the righteous, but sinners." Only the most thoroughly smug could have missed the irony.

It was not the first time, nor the last, that Jesus was reproached by the ranking, respected peers of his community for the liberality of his associations. He was an unreserved mixer. He snubbed no one. "Condemn not, and you will not be condemned," he taught. "Forgive, and you will be forgiven."

He fraternized with all kinds and classes—the powerful, the rich, the outcasts, the despised Samaritans, the Roman legionnaires, the pagan Greeks and Phoenicians, learned Pharisees, tax grafters, lepers, harlots, and children. He was a most comradely man. He had a yen for people. And he observed that overstepping the conventional bounds of compatibility to consort freely with those outside it rankled the circumspect, no matter how you went at it—whether in his own glad way, or like his solemn forerunner, the austere, ascetic John the Baptist. "For John came neither eating nor drink-

ing, and they say, 'he has a demon,' " Jesus noted. "The
Son of man came eating and drinking, and they say,
'Behold, a glutton and a drunkard, a friend of tax col-
lectors and sinners'."

He made up a humorous verse about it, alluding to
the children's games of "funerals" and "weddings" and
the pouting children who wouldn't play either. Whether
the mood was light or somberly dramatic, the peevish
wouldn't approve. As Jesus put it: "We piped to you,
and you did not dance; we wailed, and you did not
weep." As for his own approach, he likened it to a
joyous wedding celebration, at which he was the bride-
groom, and at which friends were supposed to be happy.

Among intimates, he savored warm, relaxed conversation. Once at the home of Martha and Mary, when
the older sister grew upset about preparing supper and
fumed at Mary for sitting immersed in talk with Jesus
instead of helping in the kitchen, he minimized the distractions. "Martha, Martha," he soothed, "you are
anxious and troubled about many things." But personal
communication mattered more than things impeding it.
"Mary has chosen the good portion, which shall not be
taken from her."

Another time, when his own assistants tried to chase
off children flocking around him, he grew indignant.
"Let the children come to me, and do not hinder them."
Although never angering at affronts to himself, he flared
at disregard of others, particularly the neglected, and
children were widely victimized in that age.

He lifted them in his arms, caressing and blessing
them. "To such belongs the kingdom of God." They
had a candor, a wondering receptiveness and natural
trust, unspoiled by pedantry or the self-sufficient pose
of adults. "Truly, I say to you, whoever does not receive the kingdom of God like a little child shall not
enter it."

Yet his was no condescending companionship, but
rather an open, unstinted affection, flowing out to those

around him, whatever their condition. And it drew barbs, "He is mad ... possessed of Beelzebub ... a Samaritan!" He had, in fact, held a long searching discussion with a Samaritan prostitute at Jacob's well, despite his countrymen's keen contempt for any of that race. His disciples were shocked. So was she, when he spoke to her. "How is it that you, a Jew, ask a drink of me, a woman of Samaria?"

But her brittle, jaded pose melted as they talked and she poured out her secret miseries, mistakes and yearnings. Afterward, she went off singing a new confidence —a tainted woman who became the first of her sex known to win converts to Christ.

"For God sent his Son into the world, not to condemn the world, but that the world might be saved through him."

Not that he condoned the vise and exploitation around him, but he took people as they were, whatever their frailties. And by their being accepted in love, instead of meeting the usual rejection, they were changed.

Although he spent much time with the illiterate masses of the land, the despairing amharetz, he also attracted the wealthy intellectual and devoutly studious Pharisees, including the venerable Nicodemus. "Rabbi," Nicodemus addressed Jesus, counting him in the learned tradition of the Pharisees, "we know that you are a teacher come from God." However, Nicodemus, Joseph of Arimathea, the Great Gamaliel, and other noted Pharisees sympathetic to Jesus' cause in Jerusalem's council, the Sanhedrin, were outnumbered by the impious Saducees, collaborators with Rome's military rule.

Jesus also unashamedly sought out the lonely and despised. In front of a crowd in Jericho, he called out to Rome's rich, hated chief tax collector, Zacchaeus, a short, dumpy man who had climbed a tree to watch. "Zacchaeus, make haste and come down, for I must stay at your house today." The crowd muttered disdainfully. But before Jesus left, that grasping household gave way to warm benevolence. ". . . The Son of man came to seek and save the lost."

Once at the house of Simon, among the Pharisees with whom Jesus dined repeatedly, as they lay propped on their elbows around the table, eating and conversing, a desperate prostitute wandered in. She fell on her knees, wiped Jesus' feet with tear-drenched hair and anointed his head with expensive oil. The diners, recognizing the notorious woman, were aghast. "Simon," Jesus said, "I have something to say to you." "What is it, teacher?"

Jesus told a story of a creditor to whom one man owed 500 denarii and another owed 50. The creditor forgave both their debts. "Now which of them will love him the more?" Simon, who had not observed the usual courtesies extended to a respected guest by anointing Jesus' hair or supplying water for bathing his feet, hesitated and then said, "The one, I suppose, to whom he forgave more."

"You have judged rightly." Jesus turned to the woman. "Her sins, which are many, are forgiven, for she loved much; but he who is forgiven little, loves little."

6.
The Storyteller

He could turn a tale. And it left its mark. It was an old rabbinical technique, the *marshal*—the concrete, simple story about human activity that climactically lit up an idea. Jesus was a master of it.

"No man ever spoke like this man," his critics conceded. In homes, on mountainsides, at night beside campfires, on a bench in the Temple court, on lakesides, in synagogues, in streetside encounters, the Galilean spun yarns with spark, verve and permanent point. And he did it buoyantly.

"Be of good cheer," he kept telling the crestfallen. "Take heart, my son." Despite the travail he eventually endured, and the consequent melancholy portraits of him, he actually was an optimistic man. "Let not your hearts be troubled." He didn't fret. "And which of you by being anxious can add one cubit to his span of life?"

Pointing toward the brilliant, delicate anemones decorating the valley of Esdraelon, he exulted: "Consider the lilies of the field, how they grow, they neither toil nor spin; yet I tell you, even Solomon in all his glory was not arrayed like one of these." He drew a thought from that, too. "But if God so clothes the grass of the field . . . will he not much more clothe you, O men of little faith? Therefore do not be anxious . . . Let the day's own trouble be sufficient for the day."

To explain his mission, he used such plain, earthy realities—the commonplace circumstances and situations which, if given the close observation which he gave them, take on a sunburst of meaning. "What do you think?" he would begin, and then he would tell a story.

"A man had two sons . . . The man told each of them, 'Son, go and work in the vineyard today.' The first said, 'I will not,' but he went anyhow. The other said, 'I go, sir,' but he didn't. Which of the two did the will of the father?" It was absolutely clear. No matter how noble a person's professions or fine his religious claims, it was his performance that mattered, and even the outwardly defiant and doubtful might actually serve more constructively than the avowedly dutiful. "Not every one who says to me, Lord, Lord, shall enter the kingdom, but he who does the will of my Father. . . ."

He told a related story of a king whose invitations to a banquet were rejected by presumably proper friends who begged off with flimsy excuses. So the king struck them off his list and brought in masses of unkempt strangers.

His vocabulary had a picturesque zip and vividness to it. "Sift you like wheat . . ." or "blind guides, straining out a gnat while swallowing a camel." The images glowed. "Brood of vipers . . ." he once snapped when given a warning from the puppet ruler, Herod Antipas.

Although a man of his time and culture, using parabolic metaphors, alliterations, parallels, and antithesis which found a natural response in Jewish intuition, he had a style and inventiveness of his own. And it intrigued his contemporaries, including the intellectuals. "Who is this Son of man?" "He is a good man." "No, he is leading people astray." "This is really the prophet." "This is the Christ." He puzzled them. "How is it this man has such learning?" He didn't couch his message in the abstract generalities or deductive syllogisms of Greek logic, but rather in real life narratives, involving people, their surroundings and problems, so as to illuminate basic principles.

Seated on a shady hillside, watching travelers passing on the Jericho Road, he would, there or elsewhere, soon be unwinding a story. "A man going on a journey called his servants and entrusted to them his property. . . . "It went on, lean, brisk, packed with action, about how two of the servants put their portions to productive use, while the third hid his endowment and let it lie dormant. The returned master ousted him and promoted the other two.

Jesus applied the lesson to men's responsibility for using abilities given them in furthering God's creation —so as to be part of its fulfillment. "Well done . . . enter into the joy of your master." To illustrate the development of that ultimate destiny, he compared it to yeast working in dough, to a tiny seed growing and spreading, always a hidden thing, a secret germ of the divine working among men, gradual and sure, not dependent on them, yet demanding their cooperation.

His subjects ranged widely—farming, family life, lawsuits, wealth, poverty, lending, borrowing, management, labor, criminals, weddings, kings, soldiers and slaves—drawn in dramas of fear, love, betrayal, duty, hate, courage, and sometimes comedy. There must have been an amused twinkle in his eyes when he used that hugely inflated hyperbole about it being "easier for a camel to go through the eye of a needle than for a rich man to enter the kingdom of God."

Humor shows in the story of the unprincipled judge, from whom a widow kept demanding settlement of her case. He repeatedly refused, but her persistence defeated him. Sighed the judge: "Though I neither fear

God nor regard man, yet because the widow bothers me, I will vindicate her, or she will wear me out. . . ."

The point here, urging patient confidence in prayer, lay in a striking contrast. Even if a lax judge will finally respond to perseverance, how much more will "God vindicate his elect who cry to him day and night?"

Asked once why he used parables, Jesus said it was so people would sense the truth even though not fully comprehending it. He gave it a genially tolerant touch. "So that they may indeed see but not perceive, and may indeed hear but not understand." They would get the practical implications even if not the underlying principle.

He had an abundant store of material from imagination and experience. About forty different stories are recorded, but there must have been many more, since the Gospels were set down from notes and memory about thirty years afterward.

The rabbinical mashal, besides using the parable to offer specific life incidents to express a moral point, also included opening and closing questions to get hearers' thought processes involved in the issue. Jesus regularly used the ploy. "Now tell me . . ." "What man of you . . .?" "Do you see those great buildings . . .?" It was a play of questions that introduced one of his most famous parables.

A lawyer asked, "Teacher what shall I do to inherit eternal life?"

Jesus asked back, "What is written in the law?" The lawyer replied: "You shall love the Lord your God with all your heart . . . and soul . . . strength, and your neighbor as yourself." "You have answered right," Jesus said.

So Jesus, as usual, told a story—about a traveler, stripped and beaten and left on the roadside half dead. Great citizens of his own nation passed him by, but a despised Samaritan treated his wounds, took him to an inn and paid for his care. Who, asked Jesus, "proved neighbor to the man?" The answer, as always, was inescapable. "The one who showed mercy."

"Go thou and do likewise." Feed the hungry, give drink to the thirsty, welcome the stranger, clothe the naked, attend the naked, attend the sick, visit the sick, visit the prisoner. "Truly, I say to you, as you have done it unto the least of these my brethren, you did it to me."

His deep note of joy showed in other memorable parables—of the shepherd's happiness at finding a lost sheep, a woman's delight at finding a lost coin, a father's celebration over the return of a prodigal son. Jesus, who saw his own work as restoring the lost and the prodigal, said, "It was fitting to make merry and be glad for your brother was dead and is alive; he was lost and is found."

7.
An Ambitious Aunt

She was daring, venturesome, idealistic, brimming with energy. She was a woman of property. She apparently was ambitious and something of a firebrand. She also was Jesus' aunt.

The fraternal Galilean linked himself by intention with the downtrodden, the poor, the pursuers of peace and justice. Not all of his relatives condoned his chosen involvements.

But his aunt did. She did so with majestic expectations, and eventually, with sobered realism. She stuck close to him during the three years of his swift, momentous ministry, and was among the well-off women who, as reported in Luke 8:30, financed it "out of their means." She was sure of the cause, even though she brashly misconstrued it, while many of his hometown relatives plainly doubted it. She pressed advice on him. She refused to abandon him even when danger drove most of his apostles away.

Salome was true-blue family. A typical sort of rich

aunt, aggressive, strong-minded, meddlesome, but un-
swervably loyal to her own. Her name, although vari-
ants are possible, is indicated by comparing John 19:25
which lists Jesus' "mother's sister" in a group of women
and Mark 15:40 which lists "Salome" instead in the
same group.

Elsewhere, in Matthew 27:56, Salome is identified as
"the mother of the sons of Zebedee"—James and John,
who were among the apostles of Jesus, presumably
cousins. He nicknamed the high-strung pair "sons of
thunder." The designation fit. The young men were
fireballs of emotion and drive. They came from a comfortable household. Tall walls and pleasant arbors
rimmed the courtyard of the Zebedees. In their great
stone house in Bethsaida, on the north shore of the Sea
of Galilee, the many chambers gleamed with hanging
lamps, rich carpets, curtains, and couches.

Zebedee owned a fishing business with hired employees, a fleet of vessels, and doubtlessly a packing
plant where the fish were salted down in casks for sale
to freight caravans on the Damascus trade route. It was
a substantial industry compared to the humble lot of
the kinfolk in Nazareth, about thirty miles to the
southwest.

Salome valued prestige, the leverage of class and
possessions. It was the coin of world power and she was
a practical woman. But she was also socially concerned,
a staunch Israelite, with strong feelings of nation and a
compassion for its people. Yet she and the hardheaded
Zebedee must have been shaken when their two sons
quit the profitable family enterprise to join with Jesus
in his unpredictable, nonconforming activities. James
and John, despite their material advantages, always had
looked to Jesus with such admiration for his independent spirit that they consented unhesitatingly to go
with him the moment he proposed it.

"I will make you become fishers of men," he told
them. They left immediately without a question, giving

up their comfortable security, heading into an unsettled, precarious future. It was natural for their parents to fret at such an unconventional turn in their young. After rearing them up, laying the foundations for them in occupation and resources, it was hard to see them forsake it all, going off on some rash, visionary tangent.

Zebedee, like most Jewish fathers of that time, would have counted on his sons to carry on his establishment. "O sons, listen to me," the sages of Proverbs plead. "A man's wealth is his strong city; the poverty of the poor is their ruin."

Yet Jesus' custom-shattering course plunged him into the very midst of the rabble—the beggars, the smelly tanners, the peasants, the outcast lepers, the woodcarriers, the sick, and the halt. "Blessed are you poor . . . you that hunger now, for you shall be satisfied." He had some inborn affinity with the stricken masses under the heel of imperial Roman arms and oppression. The meek, he said, "shall inherit the earth."

Salome sympathized, in a political sense. She, like many others stemming from the heroic House of David and its long lost glories, yearned to see the foreign usurper driven from the land and Israel's greatness restored.

Zebedee kept gruffly busy with his ships and dock hands, and whether or not he approved of it, Salome began frequenting the happenings and gatherings wrought by her nephew. She likely visited often with her sister, Mary, about it. It was a strange experience. At first, she may have been motivated by a desire to stay near her sons, but she absorbed the deeper magnetism of it, the current of powerfully rising expectancy.

She and other women of means furnished provisions and funds to sustain Jesus' itinerant company, and traveled much with it to attend its needs. Salome also was touched by the fiery dedication of her sons. They were thunderbolts, indeed.

Once, when a village of Samaritans refused hospital-

ity to Jesus, James and John advocated calling down
fire from heaven to burn the town. But Jesus rebuked
them. "The Son of man came not to destroy men's
lives but to save them." When a healer was observed
performing acts in Jesus' name, but who declined to
accompany Jesus' band, John in his zeal wanted to
prohibit the man from working alone. But Jesus would
impose no narrow exclusivism. "For he that is not
against us is for us."

Salome matched the fervor of her sons, absorbing
the crowd's excitement, the swelling intensity of the
movement. All the land churned with hope of a messiah, a new kingdom to throw off Rome's yoke. She
recognized that James and John held a special place
of confidence with Jesus, along with Peter. John especially was the disciple that Jesus loved.

In anticipation, she went to him with her sons, as
related in Matthew 20, saying she had a special request
to make of him. He was readily attentive. "What do you
want?" She put it bluntly, like an elder counselor accustomed to being heeded. "Command that these two
of mine may sit, one at your right hand and one at your
left, in your kingdom."

It seemed entirely reasonable to her, considering not
only the family connection, but also the able diligence
of her sons. It also was sound organizational planning
to get major cabinet officers picked in advance. Jesus
looked fondly at his aunt, and slowly shook his head.
"You do not know what you are asking." He turned to
James and John. "Are you able to drink the cup that I
am to drink?"

Always eager, not realizing the crucifixion he faced,
they said, "We are able." His expression clouded, and
he nodded. "You will drink my cup." Indeed they
would. James was slain by the collaborationist regime
to become the first martyred apostle, and John was arrested, then exiled to a desolate island.

But Jesus didn't give the details. He said that the

kind of passing political power proposed by Salome was not his to grant, that relationships would be settled in the divine province. The implications didn't seem to impress them. The rest of the apostles, similarly preoccupied with potential governing status, were indignant that Salome had tried to curry special privilege for her sons.

Jesus interceded in the quarrel, seeking to make clear that his domain was not to be run like Rome's empire—by force and domination. "You know that the rulers of the gentiles lord it over them and . . . exercise authority over them," he said. "It will not be so among you." He eyed them for a few moments, and went on. "Whoever would be great among you must be your servant, and whoever would be first among you must be your slave; even as the Son of man came not to be served but to serve, and to give his life as a ransom for many."

Salome was silent. She had miscalculated the kind of community he was building. Somehow it would be a mutually reciprocating sort of realm, a society of unreserved, mutual generosity—not ruled by mastery, rank, or superiority. These usual trappings of power had meant much to her. A sensible, direct woman, she had thought Jesus would achieve his sovereignty in these ordinary ways.

When he gained, not a crown, but a cross, she was among the few who stayed with him to the finish—some women, including her sister, Jesus' mother Mary, and only John among the apostles. It was a last family request when he asked John to care for Mary. "Behold, thy mother."

Things hadn't turned out as Salome had expected or wanted. But whatever kind of dynasty Jesus was establishing, she believed in it. It would be a good one, including all those unfortunate sufferers he equated with himself. He would build a bigger, nobler line. She could depend on it. After all, he was her nephew.

8.
The Zealot Apostle

A curtain of silence surrounds his role. He is named but not characterized. No word of his is recorded. His ways, attitudes, and activities are unmentioned. But his party instigated revolution. He also was one of the twelve. Jesus deliberately chose him as an apostle— Simon the Zealot.

That designation, "a Zealot," is the only information specified about him in Scripture, but the accounts were set down at a time when fuller published details could have brought Christians under even harsher repressions by the Roman empire. For the disturbing fact was that the Zealots had fanned a massive rebellion for independence crushed only by Rome's total destruction of ancient Israel.

"No master but God!" they vowed in resisting the alien pagan regime. They circulated clandestinely in Jerusalem, meeting behind locked doors, and formed guerrilla bands in the outlying hills to strike at the Roman oppressor. "They have an inviolable attachment to liberty, and say that God is to be their only ruler and Lord," writes Flavius Josephus. He adds that they were indifferent to "any kind of death, nor indeed do they heed the tortures of their relations and friends, nor can any such fear make them call any man Lord."

The empire, however, asserted the lordship of Caesar. Despite the risks involved, the gospel writers themselves included oblique, uncritical references to the mounting resistance and also made clear Jesus' own intensifying conflict with the ruling establishment.

It was a period of pervasive unrest, of factional polarization, smouldering discontent, protests, flaring aspirations, disorders and violence, similar in some ways to the strife of the modern age. "The truth will make you free," Jesus said. "The time is fulfilled and the kingdom of God is at hand," he proclaimed as his ministry began, the apocalyptic ring in his words pointing to some fundamental, coming change in the existing order.

It was a sizzling theme. Thousands of poor peasantry of the land, the Amhaarez, mistakenly expected him to himself lead a movement to break the foreign yoke and restore sovereignty to God's elect nation. "The Spirit of the Lord is upon me, because he has appointed me to preach good news to the poor," he declared in his first sermon. "He has sent me to proclaim release to the captives . . . to set at liberty those who are oppressed."

Alarmed hometown neighbors in Nazareth, which was traversed by a road used regularly by Roman patrols in Galilee, forcibly hustled him out of the village. He later told his men: "Behold, I send you out as sheep in the midst of wolves; so be as wise as serpents and innocent as doves . . . When they persecute you in one town, flee to the next . . . And do not fear those who kill the body but cannot kill the soul."

Besides the Zealot, some of his other apostles were passionate, temperamental men, including the impetuous Peter. Two others, James and John, called "sons of thunder," once suggested burning a village that refused to receive Jesus. "Lord, you want us to bid fire come down from heaven and consume them?" they asked. He rebuked them for it.

His own attitude toward the flames of insurrection rising around him is never precisely delineated in the biblical narratives. Indeed, he stressed peace, tenderness, forbearance. Yet, there also are reassuring notes of perilous initiatives. "I came to cast fire on the earth, and would that it were already kindled!" he declared. "Do you think I have come to give peace on earth? No, I tell you, but rather division." He indicated the struggle would be between the committed and the indifferent.

There also were oblique allusions to the spiraling national conflict. Apparently referring to Rome's eventual degradation of the Temple by fire, pillage and heathen sacrifices there, Jesus is quoted in Mark 13:14: "When you see the desolating sacrilege set up where it ought not to be (let the reader understand) then let those who are in Judea flee to the mountains." The mountain caves served as hideaways of the Zealot bands.

Mark's veiled parenthetical comment suggests the dangerous pressures under which he wrote for believers in Rome, where tradition says he gathered material from the apostle Peter before he was executed in 64 A.D. But just what relationship, if any, did Jesus have with those relentless Zealot fighters for faith and freedom? The answer in the New Testament documents is obscure, perhaps purposely so, considering the precarious status of Christians then.

Yet the silence itself speaks. Although the record contains sharp criticisms by Jesus of other major factions of the time, especially the Rome-controlled collaborationist Temple hierarchy, not a word is set down against the Zealots. They constituted a fiery, spreading underground in the populace, unswervingly dedicated to preserving God's covenant uncompromised by submission to the heathen military domination.

"They are men of great courage and spirit who are willing to die in defense of their national customs and laws with unshrinking bravery," wrote Philo, the Alexandrian Jewish philosopher. "Zealots for the Torah," they're sometimes called, resembling a phrase used in Acts 21 to describe the founding Christians in Jerusalem. Seemingly, if he ever had repudiated the Zealot cause, the Gospel writers would have noted it, since this might have made life safer for Christians and allayed Roman suspicions that they were subversives.

Instead, however, the accounts simply mention, tersely and without elaboration, that Jesus picked a Zealot as one of his apostles, his closest companions, heirs to his mission and builders of his church. Some interpreters suggest the Zealot previously had quit the incendiary movements, but the Gospels don't say so. Tracing the various clues, British historian-theologian S.F.G. Brandon concludes that a "bond of common sympathy must have existed between them.

"The profession of Zealots had evidently been compatible with a close association with Jesus," Brandon says. But they pursued different courses. Both emphasized the absolute sovereignty of God and sided with the victimized poor against the depredations of the mighty. But the Zealots advocated armed revolt, forcible overthrow of the occupation government. Their movement had antecedents in the time of the Maccabees, who in 164 B.C. unleashed a long, victorious guerrilla war against the Syrian empire's attempts to impose idol worship. Even further back in Moses' time, as told in Numbers 25, the ancient Zealot prototype, Phinehas, tried to stop intrusion of Moabite idolatry in Judaism.

However, the new wave of uprisings began in 6 A.D. when Rome ordered a tax census for instituting collection of tribute from the subject population, as was imperial policy in other conquered provinces. Already

Judea seethed with bitter hostility toward Roman rule. Just two years before, 3,000 citizens were slain by troops in a melee in Jerusalem. Rome seized control of the priesthood, naming its own religious officials, compelling daily sacrifices in the Temple in the empire's welfare.

But with the edict demanding the new tribute, a bold rabbi, Judah, and a scholarly Pharisee, Zadok, denounced it as an "introduction to slavery," urged the people to "assert their liberty" and lit a chain of revolution. "Thus did a great and wild fury spread itself over the nation," writes Josephus. Roman legions stormed through Galilee, Samaria and Judea, razing towns in bloody reprisal. About 2,000 Jews were crucified along the roadsides, another 30,000 sold into slavery. Others fled to the mountains to fight back.

Sporadically, with rising fury, the turmoil continued into the period of Jesus' ministry and beyond it, moving toward the eventual cataclysm in 66 A.D. Numerous Zealot leaders, Jacob, Simeon, Menahem, Athronges, Eleazar, Theudas, an Egyptian Jew, some claiming to be the Messiah to bring godly rule, gathered fighting men in the wilderness, striking at the heathen government. Again and again, Roman legions swept the countryside, beheading and crucifying ringleaders, slaughtering their followers, clapping thousands into chains to slave in the quarries. Troops of Pilate repeatedly smashed upheavals with savage brutality.

Once, questioners sought to trap Jesus into either an open avowal of defiance against the hated tribute tax or into servile endorsement of it by asking him whether citizens should pay it. He examined a denarius, noting Caesar's image, and gave his subtle answer: "Render to Caesar the things that are Caesar's, and to God the things that are God's." The latter in Jesus' teaching as well as that of other Jewish rabbis, embraced all existence.

Some scholars have equated the Zealots with the

Qumran community, the Essenes, a militantly pious Jewish sect whose scrolls of Scripture and battle manuals were found in modern times in caves near the Dead Sea. "Be strong! Be bold! Be valorous men!" their orders exhorted. "Fear not in battle. Do not be alarmed nor tremble at them. Do not retreat . . . for they are the congregation of wickedness."

They, too, had their organized strongholds in the desert mountains. In the cities, where the Zealots had secret sympathizers, they initially operated covertly, stirring up dissent. But gradually, as the rebellion grew, they became more aggressive in the capital itself. Their tactics in the city earned them a new name, the Sicarri, or Assassins—so called for the short, crooked dagger they carried under their cloaks, the Sicca, used for hit-run assassinations of Roman officers and collaborators.

Despite the bloodshed, their driving purpose was intensely religious. They saw subservience to a divinized Caesar as disloyalty to God, and they fought to restore the kingdom to Israel. Jesus himself was tempted in the desert before his ministry began, the devil offered him glory and royal dominion, but Jesus rejected those ambitions.

"You shall worship the Lord your God, and him only shall you serve," he said. It was the same commitment as that avowed by the Zealots, but it was directed, not just at one time and place, but at everywhere, always.

9.
The Rebel

With callous, sun-darkened hands, Jesus braided the leather thongs, forming them into a long whip like that used by cattle drivers. Then the demonstration began. It was a wild scene. He struck forcefully at the country's biggest political-economic institution, the Temple trading system. It was a shocking, dangerous move, with fierce repercussions.

The money exchange and commercial transactions, operated by the Jerusalem Temple and under control of the Roman military government and the collaborationist Sadducean aristocracy, was the civic-financial hub of the Judean power structure. At it, Jesus unleashed his most vehement onslaught.

"Take these things away!" he commanded, driving the currency brokers, merchants, and livestock from the the Temple's vast outer court where the business was carried on. "You shall not make my father's house a house of trade."

He overturned tables, toppled chairs, knocked down pigeon sales booths, and upset the money chests, the various Gospel accounts relate. Coins spilled across the polished pavement, traders and customers alike, along with birds, sheep, and oxen scattered before the foray.

Stunned amazement silenced the harps and flutes of the white-robed Levite choir on the central circular stairsteps, which led up to the tall, ornamented double doors—the doors to the sacred interior. Quoting the prophet Isaiah, Jesus declared, "My house shall be called a house of prayer for all the nations." A sign on a low balustrade forbade foreigners from entering the inner courts, on pain of death. He went on, "But you have made it a den of robbers."

If he had any help, it is not specified, but his disciples were there, and the magnitude of the traffic and impact of the action suggest their involvement. In any case, the power of the person had a staggering effect. Mark's Gospel indicates that Jesus temporarily controlled movement in the entire area, blocking use of it as a shortcut for freight portage. He would "not allow anyone to carry anything" across the huge, open court, which was four furlongs (a half mile) around.

Armed Temple guards either feared to intervene, or were swept aside. From the towers of the Fortress Antonia, at the court's northwest corner, Roman sentries looked on, awaiting orders. Jesus evidently had popular support in the affair, since the infuriated Temple officials wanted him destroyed, Mark notes, but "feared him" because of the mood of the multitude.

The Gospel of John notes that the disciples, seemingly worried at the tumultuous episode and its contrast with Jesus' usual ways, found their explanation of it in a remembered Psalm 69:9: "Zeal for thy house will consume me."

Christians often try "to tone down" the incident, but it's part of the authentic character of Jesus, says theologian Arthur J. Gossip in *The Interpreter's Bible.* "The gentle Jesus, meek and mild idea has been so overworked" that the common view of Jesus "has small resemblance to the Christ of the New Testament."

It was not the first time Jesus had touched off tumult, or openly defied the ruling authorities. He lived in a time of civil disorders, of violent protests, of marches and rallies, of alienation between races and groups, of upheavals not unlike those in modern America, and he himself sometimes took drastic direct action to make a point. He also used some strong language. "Blind guides . . . fools!" he excoriated the ostentatiously pious religious leaders, preoccupied with liturgical exactitude. "Hypocrites! You are like whitewashed tombs, which outwardly appear beautiful, but within they are full of dead men's bones."

"You will know them by their fruits," he said. "Not every one who says to me, 'Lord, Lord', shall enter the kingdom of heaven, but he who does the will of my father."

Although Jesus manifested an immense tenderness, compassion, and peaceful magnanimity—even toward enemies—there was also a fiery urgency and iron purpose about him. "Follow me, and leave the dead to bury their own dead," he said. "No one who puts his hand to the plow and looks back is fit for the kingdom of God."

Far from being the mild, passive, sweetly comforting Jesus, as he is sometimes portrayed, he left a vividly different impression on the apostle John, who pictured him as an awesome, righteous judge riding a white horse. "His eyes are like a flame of fire," the apostle wrote as a prisoner on the Isle of Patmos. "He is clad in a robe dipped in blood, and the name by which he is called is the Word of God."

In his life on earth, Jesus showed that driving, unshakeable might. As a Jew, he defied racial barriers, fraternizing with Samaritans, reciting their neighborly virtue in a famed parable. He broke rules by plucking grain to eat and by healing on the Sabbath. "The Sabbath was made for man, not man for the Sabbath," he said. "It is lawful to do good on the Sabbath." He also broke the rules of ritual ablutions before meals, and snapped back at those who censured him for it.

He discomfited the rich. "Truly, I say to you it will be hard for a rich man to enter the kingdom of heaven." He needled the lawyers. "Woe to you lawyers! For you lead men with burdens hard to bear, and you yourselves do not touch the burdens with one of your fingers."

He spurned threats by Rome's Galilean puppet, Herod Antipas, to kill him. "Go tell that fox . . . I must finish my course." Already then, Jesus' forerunner, John the Baptist, had been imprisoned by Antipas, and beheaded.

In some cases, he sparked uproars that distressed him. At one time, as noted in John 6:15, after he had fed 5,000 on the mountainside, the excited acclaiming crowd was about to "take him by force to make him a king." It was an edgy situation, for Zealot rebels were pressing, by guerrilla raids and public commotions, to throw off Roman rule and restore Israel's autonomy. But Jesus sought no political throne. He broke away from the clamorous adulations and withdrew alone into the hills.

"Behold, I send you out as sheep in the midst of wolves," he had told his men two years before as they sat around a mountain campfire near Bethsaida. "So be as wise as serpents and innocent as doves." From that point onward, there was an almost martial beat in the course he followed—a steady, muffled roll of portending battle despite the calm he maintained in the face of it. "Do not fear those who kill the body but cannot kill the soul," he said. "He who finds his life will lose it, and he who loses his life for my sake will save it."

His early instructions deploying his men carried an ominous urgency. "Take nothing for your journey, no staff, nor bag, nor money." Not even a change of garment. In this task, there was no place for ordinary concerns. Eat and lodge wherever the door is open to you. No time can be wasted. If a town spurns you, "shake off the dust from your feet as you leave." Do not pause because of reverses. Press on. "But beware," he warned. Foes will encircle you and deliver you up to their councils. "But do not be anxious . . . he who endures to the end will be saved."

On another occasion, as related in Luke 12:1, the teeming throngs he drew around him became so disorderly that "they trod upon one another" Hired henchmen tried to stone him, and on occasion amid stormy street commotions, as noted in John 10:39, he escaped attempts to arrest him.

Before his blow at the Temple merchandising traffic, he had staged another public demonstration with ominously challenging implications for the reigning hegemony.

In line with the prophecy in Zechariah 9:9, that Israel's triumphant, redeeming king would come humbly and "riding on an ass," Jesus arranged to enter Jerusalem in that manner. And the populace offered a fervent, royal welcome.

Cloaks, palm branches, and flowers were strewn before him. "Hosanna!" the people cried. "Blessed be the king who comes in the name of the Lord! Blessed be the kingdom of our father David that is coming! Hosanna in the highest!"

The whole city was stirred up, Matthew says. Fellow rabbis advised him to disavow the public exaltation of him and rebuke his followers, but he said, "I tell you, if these were silent, the very stones would cry out." He let the rapturous celebration roll and reverberate. Then came the thrust at the Temple power center and the Rome-run sacerdotal aristocracy.

Jesus was not protesting Temple worship, which he himself and his followers practiced, but rather its corruption. Roman rulers had dominated it for twenty-five years through a subserviently cooperating, wealthy

Sadducean party, which supervised the priesthood and personnel.

The Roman governor appointed the chief priests, an office then held by Caiaphas, insisted on daily sacrifices to the Roman emperor's well-being, even kept Temple vestments in Rome's Fort Antonia. Pontius Pilate once seized the Temple treasury for an aqueduct project, stirring a mass protest demonstration, put down by troops with wanton slaughter.

The trading system had become a huge, highly lucrative industry, involving Jerusalem's main monied interests and magnates, employing 120,000 priests in 24 relays, and hundreds of others. Although the markets and financial exchange provided a convenience to worshipers in obtaining unblemished animals for sacrifice and the half-shekel Hebrew coins required for tithes, fee-gouging, graft, and profiteering evidently had become common, in addition to the patronage pressures exerted by Rome.

Ancient rabbinic writings of the Talmud tell of corruption and greed existing in the Temple's operations in that period, and historian Josephus says that the Sadducean hierarchy embezzled the revenues, while ordinary priests went hungry. The scholarly Pharisees scorned the pro-Roman Sadducees, and their disbelief in an afterlife, or a personal relationship with God, or even the worth of individual ethics.

It was at this defiled, misused institution, which was supposed to represent the best impulses, hopes, and integrity of his people but which instead had become a vehicle of national compromise and exploitation, that Jesus directed his impassioned assault. "There will not be left here one stone upon another, that will not be torn down," he said. "Destroy this Temple, and in three days I will raise it up."

Those words would be used to convict him of threatening violent destruction against the state, although, as John 2:21 notes, he referred to the temple of his own life, as the cornerstone of existence, although few then understood it.

Quoting Psalm 118:22-23, he said,, "The very stone which the builders rejected has become the chief cornerstone. This is the Lord's doing and it is marvelous in our eyes."

He had been rejected by the establishment and by his hometown. Even his own relatives tried to restrain him from his course, considering it mad. The conventional denounced him as a Beelzebub.

But Jesus, who never confined himself to safe spiritual philosophizing, drove ahead, taking definite stands and forthright actions, knowing it would put him in jeopardy. And the Sadducean collaborators felt the leverage of Rome ready to respond to it. "If we let him go on thus, everyone will believe in him, and the Romans will come and destroy both our places and our nation."

Jesus saw where it all led. "If any man would come after me, let him deny himself and take up his cross daily and follow me." The Zealots, thousands of whom had been crucified, had made the cross a sign of martyrdom for Israel's freedom even before Jesus made it a symbol of deliverance for all men. "For whoever would save his life will lose it, and whoever loses his life for my sake, he will save it."

10.
The Comforter

Deep ravines trenched the mountainsides, and out of them burst the sudden storm. Ranging all around, on every side, the dark, brooding defiles of the winds disgorged their intermittent fury on the sunken sea. And men traveled on that sea.

It was a treacherous place to be, unpredictable, chancy, so placid one moment, so wild the next, with shrieking violence and panic. Mortals trembled at it. Was there no security, no certitude, on this nether passage? Was God asleep, or dead? "Do you not care if we are perishing?" the apostles cried.

Down from the corrugated heights, which rim the Sea of Galilee, the funnel-like gorges spew their instant squalls on that yawning waterway, 700 feet below sea level. And the voyagers saw no hope. It was night. The boat plunged and rolled, swamped by the hurting waves. And the human beings, caught there in the peril and crisis native to their realm, despaired. "Master, Master, we are perishing!"

Yet despite their doubts, there also was stability in

that fierce crossing. There was basic sustenance and balance in the teeth of the tumult and frenzy among men. "Peace! Be still."

In that voice, out of the mystery of that man called Jesus, flowed overwhelming calm. "Why are you afraid? Have you no faith?" And into the savagery that lashed the earth came strangely, overruling serenity. It had seemed, in the buffeting of the elements and helplessness, that he was uninvolved, uncaring, a sleeping Lord, no longer present; but he was there, nonetheless, accessible, responsive to men's insufficiencies.

It is odd that an itinerant Jewish teacher of obscure Galilee could instill such assurance, such deep-going trust and respite into the turbulent journey of men. Yet he himself was enigmatic, extraordinary. He was a plain workman, a companionable mixer, a great storyteller, a nonconforming and uncompromising rebel. He was all of these faces and functions, but in sum, he was not just any of them.

"I am the door . . . I am the good shepherd . . . I am the way, the truth and the life." He could not be categorized, or pinned down to any conditional mold or mien. He fits no descriptive profile.

Despite all the discernible human capacities and stature he displayed, he remains, at last, beyond men's full explaining, even though he was one of them.

Yet in the countenance with which he graced this earthly sphere, with its varied expressions, one perhaps characterized him more adequately than all the rest. That was his role as a comforter—the one who relieved the anguish among men, who tamed the tempests of life.

"Peace I leave with you; my peace I give to you . . . Let not your hearts be troubled, neither let them be afraid." It was an inner reinforcement, a penetrating, healing balm that he dispensed along his way, freeing the rejected from loneliness, the depraved from their mire, the rich from shackles of wealth, the sick from their pain.

One after another, he talked with them, lifted them up. The blind came crying for sight. "Do you believe . . .?" "Yes, Lord." He touched their eyes. "According to your faith, be it done unto you."

A woman, weak with a chronic hemorrhage, was so sure of him that she thought that if she could touch his cloak, it would heal her. Her hand brushed the garment. "Take heart, daughter; your faith has made you well."

Whatever a person's view of miracles, man's sciences tell him that the greater the knowledge, the greater the knowing of ever greater unknowns, and some of the recorded acts of Jesus remain in that dimension which is expanded rather than negated by learning. A recurrent note figured in the healing incidents—faith in recovery. "Do not fear, only believe," he emphasized. "All things are possible to him that believes." "Go, your faith has made you whole."

He also dispensed, unstintingly, the medicine of loving forgiveness. Should a man forgive as many as seven times, an apostle asked. Not just seven, he said, but seventy times seven," beyond counting.

Devious opponents flung a shabby, stricken prostitute in front of him, saying the law demanded stoning her for adultery. He traced that unrecorded sentence in the sand, and told them: "Let him who is without sin among you be the first to throw a stone at her." Silent, abashed, they crept away, leaving Jesus and the woman alone. "Has no one condemned you?" "No one, Lord." "Neither do I condemn you; go, and do not sin again."

His actions had a consistency, a direction—the bringing of solace to others. A touch, a word, a firm assurance amid the plunder, poverty and slavery around him. "Blessed are those who mourn, for they shall be comforted. Blessed are the meek . . . those who hunger and thirst for righteousness . . . the merciful . . . the pure in heart . . . the peacemakers . . . for theirs is the kingdom of heaven."

He gave much, received little. He himself hungered, wearied and cried, and had none of the usual comforts. "Foxes have holes, and the birds of the air have nests; but the Son of man has nowhere to lay his head." Yet he radiated that immense comfort around him, that unruffled strength that subdues the storms when the going is rough, that steadies the rudder when the ship shudders and founders toward the rocks. "Why are you troubled, and why do questions arise in your heart? Where is your faith?" He asks in the howling wind. "Lo, I am with you always to the close of the age."

The world still navigates that precarious sea between the hills of time. And out of the gorges the thunders still break, the winds rage and the wayfarers huddle, forlorn, unsure, writhing against the night.

But in the thick of the tempest, a friend travels with men. He knows those seas. He has run the gamut. He has tread those inconstant waters himself. "Hail! Take heart, it is I; have no fear," there in that hard and convulsive pass, he mans the helm. That is the great comforter, he who plunged into man's struggles, emergencies, and tragedies, confronting the harshest blows, and knowing it would continue to be difficult.

"Truly, truly, I say to you, you will weep and lament but your sorrow will turn into joy. In the world you have tribulation, but be of good cheer, I have overcome the world."

PART 4
Lash of Caesar

1.
Pilate's First Challenge

The steady pounding of the Mediterranean against the man-made seawall blended now with another massive, surging sound—the footfalls and shouts of angry thousands. Pontius Pilate stepped to an outer balcony and clenched his lips. "Barbarians," he muttered. "These natives need a taste of Etruscan steel."

A vast horde of them poured into Rome's provincial capital at Caesarea in Judea, funneling through the gates, filling the brick streets, coverging on the newly appointed procurator's palace. Pilate sent his chamberlain to fetch the garrison military commander. From the gathering, clamorous multitude, he could hear fragments of their howling. "Abomination! . . . Down with the images! . . . No heathen idols for us!" Along the coastal road, out of the hills, they streamed, a raging, ragtag flood of them.

Pilate knew the cause of their uproar, although he hadn't expected its size and fury. He deliberately had ordered the imperial emblems hoisted in Jerusalem, bearing the venerated images of the Roman emperor Tiberius. It was time to make clear to these unruly Jews their real sovereign and lord. Pilate had acted to abolish Jewish laws against graven images by brazenly flaunting them and introducing the effigies of the deified emperor into the heart of Jewish life, their holy city of Jerusalem.

This harsh step, undertaken stealthily by Pilate's troops under cover of darkness, marked the beginning

149

of his ten-year rule over the occupied colony of Judea in 779 *Ab Urbe Condita,* "from the founding of the city" of Rome, 26 A.D. of the modern calendar. Just about this time Jesus of Nazareth started his ministry among the poor of the land. "The time is fulfilled, and the kingdom of God is at hand," he proclaimed. That kingdom was not, however, the new reign of Pontius Pilate.

On the contrary, it was part of a deep-rooted, smouldering religious fire that licked at pagan Rome's domination from the start, including Pilate, finally convulsing the land and permeating the world. Pilate was the fifth of the Roman governors that had ruled in Judea since 6 A.D., when Archelaus, a son of Rome's vassal king, Herod the Great, was deposed in a maelstrom of Jewish insurrection and replaced by prefects of the emperor himself to crush the resistance. It had continued sporadically, however, ever since.

Now the new Roman governor, picked by Tiberius to succeed Valerius Gratus, faced his first brush with native defiance. He was a tough military man, a product of Rome's conquering legions, an officer of the equestrian rank, second only to the empire's ruling senatorial aristocracy. His cognomen, Pilatus, derived from the pilum, the six-foot Roman spear.

In his new assignment, he was *procurator cum potestate* with full civil, military, and criminal jurisdiction over this province of rebellious Jews. He apparently was recommended for the post by the emperor's powerful, anti-Semitic counselor, Sejanus.

While some modern accounts portray Pilate as concerned with justice, ancient history relates three specific occasions on which he massacred large numbers of people. The Bible mentions another of his mass slaughters and a group crucifixion. He was finally recalled by the emperor for excessive cruelty. Pilate had determined on a Judean policy of iron discipline, of stern measures to impress on these constantly insurgent subjects that Rome was their master, that awe must be shown the emperor whether they liked it or not. After all, Tiberius himself had laid down the motto: "Let them hate me so long as they fear me."

A tribune, commander of Pilate's headquarters cohort, was ushered into the governor's chambers, reporting what Pilate already surmised—that a huge segment of Jerusalem's people had marched 400 furlongs (about fifty miles) to Caesarea to demand removal of the imperial standards set up in their capital city. "They contend the images of our sacred emperor are contrary to religion," the tribune went on contemptuously. "It doesn't make sense. All Jerusalem is said to be in turmoil."

"A pack of crazed jackals," Pilate mused, turning his officer's vitus staff in his fingers. A military symbol of discipline, the short, smoothed vine staff often was used on the backs of subordinates. Pilate had kept it from his legion days. "We'll twist their tails," he added.

While all the previous Roman governors had avoided offending Jewish sensibilities by keeping sculptures and other representations of Caesar out of Jerusalem, Pilate had decided to break the opposition. Using a clandestine stratagem, a kind that would mark his methods, he had the military standards bearing the emperor's likeness unfurled from the city's parapets in the middle of the night to present the Jews with a *fait accompli*.

As Rome's chronicler of Jewish life, Josephus, describes the reaction, "This excited a very great tumult among the Jews when it was day. . . . A vast number of people came running into the country. These came zealously to Pilate to Caesarea, and besought him to carry those ensigns out of Jerusalem." Pilate directed the tribune to herd the rabble-rousers into the hippodrome, if it would hold them, and set up the portable judgment seat there. Shortly, a palace guard escorted Pilate to the dais. He stood there until the throng grew quiet, and then spoke: "In the name of our sovereign lord Tiberius, emperor of the entire world, I have been empowered to rule this province of Judea-Samaria, to maintain its peace, oversee its tribunals, collect its revenues, patrol its territories and serve Caesar. We honor him openly and our military banners signify it. They will not be removed. You shall desist from this disturbance and return to your homes, or incur the wrath of Caesar."

With that, he abruptly left the platform and strode back to his villa, followed by his adjutants—and also by a rising, shocked murmuring of the crowd. He had assumed his firm stand would settle the matter. It didn't. The massed gathering stayed there, seething with relentless indignation, like some herculean, growling beast. Throughout that night and through the next day, the crowd stayed there, occasionally chanting psalms and other hymns, joining in long, rolling prayers, as deep-throated as thunder. In the intervening silences came bitter cries and hoarse threats. "Idolatry! . . . A mockery of God! . . . Smite the sacrilege!"

Pilate let them bleat and broil. They'd wear out in time, get hungry, bone-sore and disperse. But they didn't leave. They stretched out on the ground, a giant human carpet, twisting, protesting, heaving. Pilate's nerves ravelled and his wife, Claudia Procula, gave him dark, questioning stares. He was aware of these people's strange religious code forbidding any graven image for adoration. "You shall not bow down to them or serve them," their law commanded. The Jews worshiped some ineffable, unseen God that couldn't be portrayed, and as Pilate recognized, their belief rivaled the Roman state pantheon represented by the divine Caesar.

"Savage fanatics," Pilate fumed. "Undisciplined, seditious ruck. We must teach them a lesson, once and permanently." "They are firm," Procula said. "You've always praised firmness." He glared at her. They had married shortly before he was promoted to this troubled but important outpost. Judea stood at the crossroads of three continents, Asia, Europe, and Africa, a lynchpin of the empire, but it had churned with uprisings ever since Julius Caesar conquered it in 63 B.C.

No other colony in all the empire gave Rome such difficulties in maintaining control as the little, religiously impassioned stretch of peninsula along the western end of the great sea. The Jews refused even minimal allegiance to the Roman gods. The paramount duty of the procurators, as Pilate saw it, was to smother the resistance. He would not flinch from battering heads to do it.

The initial siege against him went on for five days and five nights at his seacoast headquarters city of Caesarea. The city was built in imposing Roman style, with its temple to the gods, its colossal statue of Augustus, its baths, drill fields, turreted walls, and semicircular harbor ringed by an artificially built wall of rock.

Pilate watched, and the crowd not only stayed, it grew, and so did his anger. On the sixth day he instructed the garrison's commander to post a heavy detachment of infantry, cavalry, and spearmen under the stadium galleries, and when he appeared, to surround the protesting demonstrators, awaiting his signal to unsheath their weapons. Allowing time for the preparations, Pilate strode to the outdoor platform. The troops clattered into a menacing circle around the demonstrators. He spoke coldly:

"The imperial emblems which you insult with your commotion shall not be removed, now or at any time. It would be an injury to Caesar. Your effrontery avails naught. I command you, for the last time, disband, cease this disorder!" Their rebuff slammed back at him. "Down with them! Down with the profanations! No defilement of the holy city!" He stepped back and signaled to the tribune. With a clanking of metal, the troops unsheathed their weapons. "You will be cut to pieces if you do not submit at once and leave off this disturbance," Pilate warned.

Madly, unitedly, as if with one singularly wild mind, they knelt down and bared their necks, inviting the drawn blades. "We would rather be slain than transgress our law and our God," one shouted. Others joined in the reckless defiance, tilting their bared necks. Pilate stiffened, the veins hardening around his eyes. "We would rather be slain ..." They were like lambs in a slaughter pen, helpless, yet daring him. He hesitated. A gesture, and they would die.

Yet he feared having his first report to Tiberius tell of his massacre of an unarmed, unresisting crowd. It would make him look shakily impetuous. He didn't mind their dying, but he coveted his rising career. He drew in his breath and blared at them: "I was merely testing your seriousness. The standards will be removed."

A roar of jubilation went up as he stormed off the platform frustrated, furious. Next time it would go differently, and deadlier. But he would have to work from the inside, not from a lofty distance. He still would Romanize these beggars. But he himself had learned a lesson about handling them.

2.
Plotting His Power

Music of flutes, timbrels and lyres emanated from the eastern hill overlooking Jerusalem and Pontius Pilate, having a backrub in his rooftop solarium, glanced up, squinting into the sun. Another flock of rural peasants, he assumed, invading this already overpacked city for their religious frolic.

These affairs, particularly the big one called Passover, usually meant trouble for the Roman occupation government and Pilate regularly brought extra troops from Caesarea to the city's garrison at the Fortress of Antonia to keep down any threatening disorder. For the moment, however, he was at ease. He had discovered how to control these obstinately intractable Jews and the system worked, even though he had to lop off some rash heads now and then.

The hillside melodies faded and Pilate relaxed again, his skin tingling as his manslave drew the bone strigils to and fro. Pilate had been here about three years now, and except for that one jolting reprimand from Tiberius, he had shrewdly consolidated his power, especially in firming up his working alliance with the Temple chieftains. It was an astute arrangement, though personally irksome. They were useful to him.

They seemed about as adamant as he against the various Sicarii revolutionaries and other provocateurs and dissenters, including that one from Galilee called Jesus, with his bids to the poor, his promises of release to the captives, to set at liberty those who are oppressed under the banner of some fuzzy notion of a kingdom of God.

"A puzzling one," Pilate's wife, Procula, had once commented. "A braying jack," Pilate had said. A wild talker, indeed, even more reckless than his forerunner, the baptizer, John. The baptizer had been nuisance enough, Pilate reflected, even luring some of Rome's legionnaires to hear him before his beheading.

But things seemed quiet enough for the time being. Pilate took satisfaction in the way he had tightened lines of support with the powerful and monied Temple managers. Their collaboration was not paraded openly. It couldn't be, and fine for that, he mused distastefully.

No Jew could remain acceptable to his fellows if he so much as supped with Romans, entered their dwellings, or even clasped their hands. A native's customary attitude was to turn his back at the sight of a Roman helmet and spit.

Consequently, Pilate and the Sadducean high priest, Joseph Caiaphas, had to work together in secret. Their tie was obvious, however, to any thoughtful observer, since the chief religious post was subject to the governor's appointment. Indeed, Rome had ousted four successive high priests before finding a sufficiently cooperative one in Caiaphas. Moreover, so closely did the foreign Roman overload and the Temple aristocracy collaborate that funds from the Temple's sacred corban were secretly relayed to Pilate for a building project. He frowned slightly, remembering the bloody riot that eventually erupted when word of it got out.

It had gone smoothly at first, though. The Temple overseers supplied the funds and Pilate had his architects and engineers begin constructing a flumed aqueduct fifty-four furlongs in length (seven miles) from springs at Bethlehem to Jerusalem's huge underground reservoirs beneath the Temple. Pilate had calculated that it would boost his status with the emperor to expand the city's inadequate water system while, at the same time, keeping imperial tax tribute flowing unabated into Rome. A shrewd move. But then, knowledge of the transfer from the Temple treasury somehow had slipped out, and a storm broke loose.

Popular indignation swept the city, Jews were outraged that the heathen Roman oppressor would get hands on the shekel tithes given for their Temple in worship of God. They had vented their fury on Pilate. "Many tens of thousands of people came together, and made a clamor against him," Josephus writes. "Some of them also used reproaches and abused the man, as such people usually do."

"Infidel plunderer!" they cried, shaking their fists

outside the governor's praetorium. "Thieving tyrant!"
Even the normally heavy Roman levies, in land tax,
grain and livestock tax, head tax and custom duties,
were bitterly resented by the subjugated peoples, even
though paid in Roman commercial coins and not the
sacrificial shekels offered at the Temple. To divert these
holy funds to pagan purposes was seen as profanation.

"Robber of the Lord!" the protesters shouted.

By the time of this upheaval, however, Pilate's position had been thoroughly shored up through power over
Temple officials. Without them, he could never even
have obtained the money from the Temple treasury,
since it was a capital offense for any Gentile, including
Romans, to enter beyond the Temple's outermost court.
When the crowd had refused to disperse, he had quickly
resorted to force and also to some of his typically
deceptive tactics. He had directed four centuries of 400
soldiers, disguised as Jewish civilians but armed with
swords and clubs hidden under their cloaks, to mingle
with the demonstrators. At his signal, they were to
lay on.

When again the mob refused to disperse, he thrust
his vitus staff upward and the troops went to work.
They "equally punished those that were tumultuous and
those that were not," Josephus recounts. Cries, moans,
and the crunch of the blades turned the scene into mass
panic. "There was a great number of them slain," the
account shows. "'Many of them were trodden to death
. . . Others of them ran away wounded. The shock at
the horrible fate of the casualties brought the people to
silence."

Around Pilate's praetorium, the grounds and streets
ran with blood, littered with struggling or inert bodies.
The slaughter had been worse than he had intended,
he recalled now, but it had thoroughly proved his
authority. No question about that. He smiled wanly. He
could not have backed down again, as he had done in

the face of that outburst at Caesarea when he first took office. The punishment had been brutal, but effective.

"How can you justify it?" Procula had demanded.

"I don't need to. Power justifies itself."

Pilate dismissed the masseur and swung off the cushioned table. A dresser brought his tunic and toga, slipped the sandals on his feet, and the governor went downstairs for his noon meal. He was an ambitious, crafty man, a strict pragmatist, trained in the Roman legions, determined to exploit every opportunity for advancement. He had a taste for devious methods, as shown by his use of disguised soldiers in crushing the Jerusalem protest, by his surreptitious nighttime erection of the imperial standard in Jerusalem, by his later bloody ambush of a group of Samaritans—methods paralleling his collusion with Temple officialdom.

An Alexandrian philosopher of the times, Philo, says Pilate was a "naturally inflexible and stubbornly relentless" man who committed "acts of corruption, insults, rapine, outrages on the people, arrogance, repeated murders of innocent victims, and constant and most galling savagery." Jesus himself, in Luke 13:1, mentions "the Galileans whose blood Pilate had mingled with their sacrifices." Although details of the episode are lacking, the implication is that a number of Galileans had come to Jesusalem to make their festival offerings and while they were at worship, Pilate's troops fell on them and massacred them on the spot.

The outbreaks continued under the Roman procurators, eventually mounting into an all-out but unavailing war against the occupation regime. Pilate, following the massacre of Jerusalem protesters against his use of Temple funds, had again inflamed local feeling by having gilded shields dedicated by him to the emperor hung in Jerusalem's Herodian palace. When he spurned pleas to remove them, Herodian princes complained to the emperor Tiberius in Rome. Tiberius sent a message sharply rebuking Pilate for his "rash innovation and uncompromising manner," ordering him to remove the shields.

Dining now in the shade of a terrace awning, Pilate had finished his mushrooms and pig's liver and was sipping a goblet of wine when again his ears caught the noise of a procession on the slope entering the city's eastern gate. This time, it was a real bellringer. Pilate stepped to the balustrade, watching uneasily. A huge, ecstatic river of people lined the road into the Sheep gate, waving leafy branches, speading fronds and their own garments along the way, shouting, "Hosanna!" It meant, "Save us!" In the midst of the adulation, a bearded man rode astride a burro, a knot of men following him.

"Hosanna! Son of David! Blessed be he who comes in the name of the Lord, even the King of Israel! Hosanna in the highest!" They seemed beside themselves, enraptured at the approach of some longed-for moment, shouting those phrases implying restoration of the old Judean monarchy. Pilate tapped his vitus stick nervously on the banister.

The demonstration obviously had been organized in Jerusalem in advance to produce such an enormous turnout. This was not just a welcome of relatives to rural pilgrims. It was an extensively planned, widely supported display of Jewish yearning for a new order. Pilate sent agents into the streets to check the extent of it and the reports came back. It was the Galilean spellbinder, Jesus. "All the city is moved," the observers reported. "The world has gone after him." The governor scowled. He would have to tame this Galilean adventurer.

3.
Chaos in the City

Like scattered brush fires, the emergencies seemed to hit at various points in Jerusalem at about the same time. Roman troops already had been concentrated on one violent outbreak when Jesus made his surprise foray at the Temple. Now another matter, a secret night ambush had to be arranged. It was a hectic time for Pontius Pilate.

Planning and directing his moves from his sectarium office, the governor received a steady stream of messages and dispatched runners to military units deployed through the city. Arrests mounted. One detachment had smashed an uprising in which several died, capturing its rebel ringleader, Barabbas. It was the Jewish Passover week and the city bulged with outlanders and national religious fervor, a time that always seemed to whip native antagonism to a flashpoint.

Pilate's forehead beaded with sweat as he faced the multiplying succession of problems and rapped out orders for trying to staunch them. From turrets atop the Tower of Antonia, over-looking the Temple square and adjoining Pilate's chambers, Roman sentries watched the onslaught led by Jesus. Swinging a braided livestock whip, he overturned coin-exchange tables, merchandising booths and sheep pens, driving out the dealers, animals, tourists and watchmen alike.

Pilate, presumably informed at once of the affair, did not immediately intervene militarily, either because he lacked sufficient reserves at the moment, with troops heavily engaged elsewhere, or because the demonstration evoked such strong popular support that he deferred counteraction until he could devise circumstances more to Rome's diplomatic advantage. Artifice was his specialty, as shown on several historically recorded repressions in which he used deceptive techniques.

In any case, that the demonstration succeeded even temporarily in vacating the huge Temple plaza, always congested and doing rush business at festival time, suggests that the disruption assumed far more powerful proportions than are detailed by the gospel narratives. It was an assault on the hub of the province's financial, cultural, and religious establishment, essential to Pilate's maintenance of colonial peace and profit.

The Temple police, employed by the Rome-appointed high priest Caiaphas and regularly posted about the courtyards and porticoes of the massive sanctuary, apparently had been swept aside along with the other Temple functionaries. However, biblical accounts make clear why the Temple administrators also had withheld action against Jesus at that time. "They feared the people," the accounts say. "They feared the multitudes. They did not find anything they could do, for all the people hung upon his words." The people themselves marveled, "Is not this the man whom they seek to kill? And here he is, speaking openly, and they say nothing to him."

The Scriptures indicate that he put pressure on the Temple leaders to cooperate in dealing with Jesus or face replacement by Rome as incompetent to cope with the situation. As one remarked in John 11:48, "If we let him go on thus, every one will believe in him, and the Romans will come and destroy both our holy place and our nation." High priest Caiaphas added that it was expedient "that one man should die for the people, and that the whole nation should not perish," meaning their civil religious jurisdiction under Roman supervision.

The governor, tense and harassed by the torrent of crises, fumed at the confused, changing reports brought to him in a constant round of briefings and decision. Repeatedly, he cut his aides off short, questioning, upbraiding, demanding further steps to shore up security and implement plans. To him, the whole city, with its strange religious passions, seemed an utter madhouse, a bedlam of discordant factions and uncertainties: steaming holiday crowds, dust, hawkers, reeking streets, rickety freight carts, bleating animals and that festering tent city of thousands outside the walls, camping out there in a dingy glut of smoke, smells and undoubtedly incendiary conversations.

Slapping his vitus staff on the table before him, Pilate ordered additional patrols around that rustic encampment, many of its occupants being hot-tempered, revolutionary hill folk. So far as he could make out from the information brought him, the flareup of revolt instigated by Barabbas was thoroughly repulsed with an unknown number of casualties. Barabbas, son of a rabbi, and other surviving insurrectionists were in prison. Mark's Gospel, in noting their capture, does not specify their numbers.

The scene of the uprising remained a danger zone, however, and Pilate kept extra troops posted there. Whether any Zealots were involved in Jesus' short-lived takeover of the Temple square is not stated. In any case, armed insurgents and fighters against Rome were among those filling the jails of Jerusalem as that Passover week neared its climax.

With some relief, Pilate noted that the Temple square had quieted down and returned to some semblance of normalcy. His main concern now was to avoid further outbursts in the keenly volatile atmosphere, in part by covertly and quickly silencing the fiery, crowd-swaying Jesus. The saving "messiah," some called him,

"Christos," the "anointed," implying some royal mantle dangerous to Rome. He claimed some special kinship to the Jewish God. Peasant throngs in Galilee had tried in vain to crown him at once—reports of which probably had reached Pilate.

An old book, the *Sybilline Oracles*, perhaps known to the Romans, contained a lengthy Jewish prayer for destruction of the heathen occupation government and anointing of a new, righteous king. "A holy king will come and reign over all the world," the prayer went. "His wrath will follow on the people of Latinum and Rome will be destroyed to the ground. O God . . . let the Romans perish . . . When will the day come . . . ?"

Pilate agreed with the high priest Caiaphas that the arrest should be made quietly with as little public notice as possible, and that the trial should be held immediately to forestall any groundswell of opposition.

4.
The Arrest

The detachment sent to seize Jesus was large enough to cope with any further armed resistance. In the heat of the encounter, there was a brief flurry of violent counteraction, quickly subdued. The apostles, at least some of them, bore arms, and stood ready to use them. "Shall we strike with the sword?" they cried, as noted in Luke 22:49. The brash, red-bearded Peter did slash out, in a furious moment of fight and flashing steel. "Put your sword back into its sheath," Jesus admonished him, and it was all over.

Battling that formidable array of Roman combat troops and Temple constabulary could only have meant annihilation for his companions, and an end to the mandate he had laid on them for the future of his mission. "For all who take the sword will perish by the sword."

It was an immemorial summons to peace, even in the face of aggression, a clear-cut, standing notice of the inevitable loss and ruin inflicted by the world's continuing scourge of armaments and war. Yet Jesus had known, even before them, of the weapons among his men, and by the record, had not objected to it.

The matter had come up as they reclined around the table in the upper room of a private house at the Last Supper, as related in Luke 22:35-38. Jesus recalled that up to then, they had traveled light, without provisions.

"But now," he said, with the changed situation hurtling toward crisis, "let him who has a purse take it, and likewise a bag. And let him who has no sword sell his mantle and buy one." The apostles, collectively, said, "Look, Lord, here are two swords." It is not specified whether they had two each, a broad sword in a side scabbard and a short dagger in the belt under the cloak, or only two among all of them. "It is enough," he said.

The fact that the apostles possessed such militant gear has been a troubling point ever since to those tending to view Jesus' ministry as all tolerance, temperance, and tranquility. He did, indeed, display an overwhelmingly insistent love, mercy and support for people, even in their faults. "Forgive and you will be forgiven," he urged. "Condemn not and you will not be condemned. Love one another."

The very heart of his mission was reconciliation, between men and God, and among one another. "Blessed are the peace-makers, for they shall be called sons of God," he said. On occasion, he urged nonresistance to abuses and assaults. "If anyone strikes you on the right cheek, turn to him the other also." "Love your enemies, do good to those who hate you, bless those who curse you, pray for those who abuse you." He wept openly over society's chronic trampling of the brave and the true. "O Jerusalem, Jerusalem, killing the prophets and stoning those who are sent to you."

But he also was a rugged man of commanding force and power. He stared down a lynch mob in Nazareth, challenged threatening stonethrowers in Jerusalem. Did you expect a "reed shaken in the wind?" he once demanded sharply about his rough-hewn colleague, John the Baptist. There was a rocklike firmness about him—a driving, unswervable purposefulness, a passion and a fire that looked threats, frustration, and danger in the eye, that moved resolutely toward his own fateful confrontation. Back in Galilee, he told his men in Luke 18:31: "Behold, we are going up to Jerusalem, and everything that is written of the Son of man by the prophets will be accomplished. For he will be delivered to the gentiles, and will be mocked and shamefully treated and spit upon: they will scourge him and kill him, and on the third day, he will rise."

Thus, the inexorable process was set in motion. From the Roman garrison at the Fortress Antonia, a large contingent of soldiers, along with Temple police, headed toward the Mount of Olives outside the city, guided by a defector from Jesus' group, Judas Iscariot, who had brought information where the accused man could be seized in isolation, so as not to stir mass public interest. His popularity with the ordinary Jewish citizenry had prevented an open arrest.

The night pulsed with apprehensions, uncertainties and smouldering hostilities. As noted in Mark 6:7, Roman troops already had rounded up a group of rebels after an insurrection in the city that involved a number of killings. John's Gospel says a cohort-size band, 600 legionnaires at full strength, was sent to arrest Jesus.

Meanwhile, he talked with his men about having

"swords," and in that same conversation, spoke of a prophecy in Isaiah 53, which he said was written about himself, a point the church only came to recognize centuries later. The passage says: "He had no form or comeliness that we should look at him, and no beauty that we should desire him. He was despised and rejected by men, a man of sorrows acquainted with grief, as one from whom men hid their faces ... But he was wounded for our transgressions, he was bruised for our iniquities, upon him was the chastisement that made us whole, and with his stripes we are healed ... the Lord has laid on him the iniquity of us all." Said Jesus: "I tell you that this Scripture must be fulfilled in me."

They headed out of the city across the Kidron valley to the east and up the mountain to an old olive press in the woods, Gethsemane. "Let not your hearts be troubled," he told them, as they walked. "Yes a little while and the world will see me no more, but you will see me: because I live, you will live also."

They reached the clearing and he told them, "Remain here, and watch." He went on a ways into the trees alone and fell to the ground, sobbing, stabbed momentarily with a sense of uncertainty and dread. "Abba, Father, all things are possible to thee; remove this cup from me; yet not what I will but what thou wilt." He cried aloud, breaking into a hot, drenching sweat that mingled with his tears. "My Father, if this cannot pass unless I drink it, thy will be done." Shortly, he rose, and awakened his drowsing men. "Behold, the hour is at hand."

Flaring lantern lights streaked through the trees, amid sounds of snapping limbs, rattling arms and many stomping feet. The forward element burst into the clearing and Judas scurried up to Jesus and kissed him, the prearranged sign to identify the wanted man. Instantly, the apostles swung to the ready, about to fight back, "Shall we strike with the sword?" Peter didn't hesitate. He whipped out his sword and slashed at the nearest target, cutting off the right ear of a man named Malchus, an aide to the high priest. Obviously there was a tumultuous, uncontrolled moment there of militantly defensive reaction, undetailed in the terse Gospel passages, but Jesus quickly intervened.

"No more of this!" he said. "Do you think that I cannot appeal to my Father, and he will at once send me more than twelve legions of angels?" He could have bested the battalion if he chose, he said, but he didn't. For, "how then should the Scriptures be fulfilled . . .?" Stunned and panic-stricken at his willing surrender, the apostles fled in frightened dismay. The troops bound Jesus' arms with ropes and led him away.

"Peace I leave with you: my peace I give to you," he had told his men earlier. "Let not your hearts be troubled, neither let them be afraid."

5.
The Trial

From his elevated, portable seat called the sella, Pontius Pilate looked down on the manacled prisoner and intoned, "Are you the king of the Jews?" It was the formal opening of a Roman trial in which the suspect was asked to reply to the charge against him. In this case, Jesus of Nazareth was accused of *crimen laesae majestatis,* injury to the majesty of the Roman emperor by illegally claiming to be king in territory of the empire. It was high treason.

"You have said so," he replied, a common Hebrew circumlocution that may be either noncommittal or imply acknowledgement. Thus, in about 29 A.D., began a judicial proceeding of immeasurable consequences. It has stirred emotions and controversy ever since. No trial in history has left so large an impact on human consciousness.

It is the stark monument to the memory of Pilate, deputy of the emperor Tiberius, governor of the imperial province of Judea, empowered with the *iu gladdi,* the right of the sword to hold the Jews in subjugation. That he set forth the specific allegation at the outset indicates his prior familarity with the case and reasons for acting on it.

But the biblical accounts also depict a raucous "multitude" clamoring for execution while a seemingly prudent governor hesitates to order it, an impression easily contrived with his Temple collaborators, and of which the accounts give evidence. "The chief priests stirred up the crowd," Mark reports. They "persuaded the multitude," John writes.

Such a maneuver squares with the designing, yet severe and domineering character Pilate displayed in other events of his administration, along with his habitual manipulations to curry favor with the emperor in pursuit of advancement. Biblical scholars also point out that the Gospels were compiled in a subsequent period when Christianity was illegal, under persecution by the empire, and to avoid fanning the flames of peril, the writers would tend to mitigate the Roman prefect's role.

In any case, the undefined "multitude" could have been only a tiny handful of Jerusalem's festival-swollen

population—more than a million according to Josephus
—and even the small pro-Roman claque on hand remained outside the walled court area. "They themselves
did not enter the praetorium," John's Gospel says, referring to the enclosed, tessellated pavement where Pilate
held court. The heathen Roman compound was considered defiling to Jews.

Those present, idlers and other factotums under
influences of the nearby Temple's Sadducean officialdom controlled by Rome, must have merely clogged
the eight-foot gateway, a knot of sensation-seekers
egged on to shout for a hanging. "We found this man
perverting our nation, and forbidding us to give tribute
to Caesar, and saying that he himself is Christ a king,"
inciters of the group said. "He stirs up the people."

Pilate leaned back with satisfaction. The high priest,
Caiaphas, installed by Rome as serviceable to its rule,
obviously had done his job of making it appear the
natives wanted a conviction, that they even respected
Caesar, despite that actual Jewish loathing for Roman
rule. It was a splendid ploy, Pilate realized, and also
mutually self-protective both for Caiaphas and Pilate.
The governor smoothed the purple hem of his toga,
gazing indifferently at the prisoner, "Have you no
answer to make? See how many charges they bring
against you." The man didn't reply.

Pilate pursed his lips, vaguely puzzled. Usually these
culprits scream out their innocence but this was a cool
one. To provide further semblance of his own impar-
tiality, Pilate dangled the idea of holiday amnesty for
one prisoner, saying: "Whom do you want me to release
for you, Barabbas, or Jesus who is called the Christ?"
The jails bulged with rebels and bandits, but special
pains had been taken to trap this one on trial, and the
bystanders, by the biblical record, were officially
coached in their answer.

"Barabas," they shot back. That should clinch it.
Pilate assumed, definitely making it look as if the *vox*

populi disowned this dangerously cryptic Jesus, although actually the common Jews so adored him that his arrest had to be in secret. That popular affection shown by pressing throngs from the moment Jesus entered the city, also had caused Pilate and his cohorts to set the trial just after daybreak before the public was aware of it.

"It was early," John writes, so early that the entire affair—which included a march across town to let Herod Antipas, Rome's tetrarch of Galilee, twit the prisoner—was over and Jesus already was on the cross by the third hour, 9:00 A.M.

That extraordinary timing, given in Mark 15:25, reveals the deliberate haste to circumvent a public outcry. Other prisoners languished in cells indefinitely before trial or execution, but Jesus was rushed through it feverishly within hours of his midnight arrest.

Cooperating Temple officials, such as Caiaphas, evidently had rounded up employees and loiterers to stage the early-morning calls for conviction before ordinary worshipers arrived in the area. Tradition locates the praetorium at the Tower of Antonia, adjacent to the Temple.

That Pilate himself would be waiting at such an early hour to pass judgment on the case strongly demonstrates his engineering of it. Also, the Temple priests would hardly have been here on their busiest Passover day except under compulsion. It was Pilate's timetable. "Then what shall I do with Jesus who is called Christ?" He put the question, knowing the answer before it came back.

"Let him be crucified."

As the heartless game continued, a clerical *apparitore* of the court handed Pilate a note. "Have nothing to do with that righteous man, for I have suffered much over him today in a dream." It came from his wife, Procula.

The governor scowled, annoyed at her introspective nature, investing mere dreams with the ominous reality of revelations. She had a perverse religious streak, even considering the Jewish idea of one divinity more sensible than Rome's multiplicity of gods.

Pilate had no use for either, except for the professional expedience of burning incense to Tiberius. Then he recalled how Calpurnia, wife of Julius Caesar, warned him because of a dream not to go to the forum on the day of his assassination. Discomfited, Pilate stood up and headed into his adjacent office, signaling the guards to bring the prisoner. There in the privacy of his curtained chamber behind the velum door hanging, he gave play to momentary curiosity. "What have you done?"

Jesus, looking straight into Pilate's eyes despite his bruises and a sleepless night of interrogation, said, "My kingship is not of this world. If my kingship were of this world, my servants would fight." This nettled Pilate, and he resumed his condescending tone. "So you are a king?"

Irony flickered in Jesus' gaze, "You say that I am a king. For this I was born, and for this I have come into the world, to bear witness to the truth."

Pilate arched his brows, snorting, "What is truth?" The interview was over. He snapped his vitus staff on the table and directed the guards to scourge the prisoner.

In the Roman *flagellatio,* condemned prisoners were flogged with a whip tipped with bone and metal before crucifixion. The troops took their time at it, and afterward draped Jesus with a scarlet sagam, a woven crown of thorns and put a reed in his hand for a mock scepter. "Hail, King of the Jews!" they taunted, laughing.

The outcome was settled, but Pilate allowed some final touches to the act after the lacerated prisoner was shoved back in front of the tribunal. "Here is the man," the governor said cynically of the weakened, bleeding Jesus. "I find no crime in him." The troopers chuckled.

The crowd reacted with mechanical deference to

Rome. "If you release this man, you are not Caesar's friend. Everyone who makes himself a king sets himself against Caesar." It was a line fit for Tiberius himself.

Pilate, jealous of his accepance into the emperor's intimate circle of official friends as *amici Caesaris,* retaliated by goading his trained seals, "Shall I crucify your king?"

"Crucify him! . . . We have no king but Caesar." It was utterly absurd, but neatly managed politics. Pilate needed his outward show of support to condemn Jesus, who gripped the hearts and hopes of so many ordinary Jews, and the governor had the power to line up his chorus.

Pilate, savoring his supremacy over the situation, offered a final bit of theatrics. Taking a bowl of water, he rinsed his hands in it, saying, "I am innocent of this man's blood." But in the end, only he could render the verdict. He could have acquitted Jesus, and by the record, it was never his nature to accede to popular demands. But in this case, he needed a pretense of it.

Now, after the spectacle, he wrote out the official *titulus qui causam poenae indicat,* specifying the convicted man's offense and reason for his punishment, so spectators would be aware of the fate of its perpetrators. The inscription read, "The King of the Jews." In Roman eyes, as Pilate judged it, Jesus threatened the might and suzerainty of Caesar, an aspiring king in treason to the empire.

He stirred so much life in the poor, so much courage in the persecuted, so much health and gladness in the ordinary people of the land that he was deemed unsafe to the masters of the world. The chief priests complained, "Do not write, 'The King of the Jews,' but 'This man said, I am King of the Jews.' "

Pilate snapped, "What I have written, I have written." He pointed his vitus staff at the prisoner, and with military crispness, gave the order to the execution detail. "Crucify him."

6.
The Aftermath

Over his head hung the official Roman *titulus* citing the crime of which Jesus had been convicted. The lettering was repeated in three languages, Hebrew, Latin, and Greek, on heavy papyrus: "The King of the Jews."

E'lo-i, E'lo-i, la'ma sabachtha'ni? he cried out loudly as he writhed on the cross, voicing in his native tongue a lonely, despairing lament of Psalm 22: "My God, my God, why hast thou forsaken me?" It was part of a prayer that devout Jews used in time of deep adversity. "I am poured out like water," it went, "All my bones are out of joint: my heart is like wax . . . melted within me . . . Thou dost lay me in the dust of death."

As the pangs of it poured through Jesus, a darkening overcast covered the Judean landscape. But even in the darkest agony, the old prayer of his people that he uttered ends on a triumphant note—and would for him. "Praise the Lord . . . He rules!"

But now, bleeding, wrenched by cramps, gasping for air, Jesus traversed the human abyss.

The wharf at Caesarea teemed with heaving porters

173

and stevedores loading the 200-foot, square-masted, merchant ship the afternoon before Pontius Pilate went aboard. He had been recalled to Rome for excessive brutality as governor of the province of Judea. A lean, rigidly erect man of military bearing, he strode hastily up the gangway, looking to neither side, followed by his wife, Procula, and a retinue of slaves and baggage.

No honor parade, no martial drums, no dipping banners of legionnaires marked his departure. Not even his successor, Marcellus, was on hand to bid him farewell. He was under a summons from the Emperor Tiberius to answer a charge of unwarranted bloodshed. Behind him he left a haunting record, including the crucifixion of Jesus.

As the ship sailed that day, Pilate emerged from the stern cabin to which he and his wife had been assigned, unable any longer to abide her estranged silence. He wove his way among the wine kegs and heaped grain sacks to an aft railing and watched the shadows purpling the hills of Judea.

"An unnatural place, he murmured. "Bewitched." It was an untamed, vehement land, each volcanic height, each whispering wind, each narrow, twisting street echoing with time, passions, and mystery. "The granddam of the Furies!" He shivered, not so much from the whiffs of damp sea air as from memories, the misty, swarming images of defiant faces, the fallen, mangled bodies, the upthrust silhouettes of laden crosses.

Those brash, spouting followers of the dead Galilean still ran amuck, spreading their tale that he lives anew and had "poured out his Spirit" for all. It even had affected Procula, ever since that eerie afternoon when the pigeon-headed centurion jabbered out his hysterical report: "Truly this was a son of God!" A twinge went through Pilate. Dimly, he heard the shouted commands of the ship's pilot as the big square mainsail of sewn hides, decorated with the Roman she-wolf and cubs, was hoisted to the full, catching wind, and driving the vessel's high prow faster toward the sinking sun.

Pilate's ramrod frame swayed with the forward pitch and his hands gripped the railing. It had not been the so-called "Christus" fever that had beaten him, not specifically anyway, yet all the rampages and retribution seemed to run together now. As for himself, in the vying ranks of imperial preference, he might be ruined, banned from further trust, even exiled.

The specific incident that had brought his downfall seemed to him a routine defensive measure, a cunningly accomplished destruction of that superstitious company headed through a mountain pass northeast of Jerusalem. Pilate, however, informed of the movement by spies, had deployed a heavy military force along the trail, concealing them in flanking ravines for an ambush. At the strategic moment, the combined force of infantry, spearmen, and cavalry fell on the unexpecting multitude and cut it to bits.

"Some of them they slew," Josephus writes. "Others of them they put to flight, and took a great many alive, the principal of which, and also the most potent of those that fled away, Pilate ordered to be slain." Roman horsemen pounded the countryside, hunting them out, executing them. A Jewish delegation had complained to the emperor Tiberius, accusing Pilate of wanton murder, insisting that the victims had not assembled in the mountain area in order to revolt from the Romans, but to escape the violence of Pilate. He was ordered to face the accusation in Rome.

Pilate put a hand to his forehead, pressing it, trying to crush the ache. Too many schemes, too many ruses, too many broken limbs, moaning victims, throttled voices and trampled liberties, too much gore.

"Father, forgive them; for they know not what they do." Procula had quoted those dying words of the Galilean to him, pleading for some sign of remorse. "Blessed are those who mourn, for they shall be com-

forted." Pilate clenched his eyes shut, remembering, remembering. The only sounds now were the slosh of
waves and the scrape of the slender wooden tillers in
their locks as the two steersmen worked in unison on
the poop-deck near where he stood.

That strange, distracting afternoon came back, that
ebbing day when the skies darkened and the ground
shook and a Temple partition tumbled, exposing the
hidden Holy of Holies.

Pilate had acceded to the request of the Jewish
council members, Joseph of Arimathea and Nicodemus,
to be allowed to take the body down and bury it, before
sunset in accordance with Jewish law, in a nearby garden
tomb. As recorded in the ancient noncanonical Book
of Nicodemus, the Roman centurion in charge of the
execution party had reported to Pilate on the crucifixion, how Jesus had died in six hours rather than the
usual twelve.

"Certainly, this man was innocent," the centurion
had blurted out. The governor, on edge because of the
sobbing of Procula, had let the impertinent remark
pass and dismissed him. Then later, in quizzing some
of his Temple collaborators, Pilate had learned of the
weird, unsettling events three days after the crucifixion
when the soldiers guarding the tomb fled in fright and
the body disappeared. "We became as dead persons
through fear," they had babbled. "We saw an angel . . .
his countenance was like lightning . . . roll away the
stone of the sepulchre . . . Jesus is risen as he foretold
. . . He truly does live."

The Temple allies of Rome had bribed the soldiers
to keep quiet about the incident and to claim that while
they slept the disciples of Jesus had ferreted away his
body. Pilate, as related in the noncanonical Gospel of
Peter, also ordered the soldiers to keep silent about
their experience. "It's the infernal heat and sorcery of
this country," he had told himself. Later, however, according to the Book of Nicodemus, he received other

reports that witnesses had seen Jesus alive after his death, and they heard him discoursing with his disciples.

The whole affair had become like a nightmare, smouldering and flaring in Jerusalem and the country-side around about, igniting deliriums among 3,000 people at the so-called Jewish Pentecost, and continuing to spread and infect the populace, despite repeated arrests of the instigators and warnings to halt their activity. Now, six years after condemning Jesus, Pilate in 36 A.D. headed back to the imperial capital in disgrace, accused of arrogant and criminal atrocities against the Jews, for a hearing before the emperor.

Night had descended over the plying Roman freighter, her large, square mainsail still bulging with the winter wind, and Pilate pulled his cloak closer about his neck. He had not heard any approach, but suddenly, he became aware that Procula stood there beside him.

"It's a lonely time," she said.

"Yes, it is."

"Whatever mistakes you've made, I still love you," she said. He turned toward her, feeling the first spark of hope in himself for a long time, and she looked up at him with pained fondness. "The God of the Jews loves you, too, despite the hurts dealt to him . . . by you, by me, by others."

He drew himself up rigidly, compressing his lips to stop their quivering. "I don't need the God sentiments," he said. "You've changed, Procula."

"Yes," she said. "I think I've found some answers, some real ones, through those followers of the Way. As they teach, Jesus was the truth, and it can clear us, make us free."

"Free? Free from what?"

"From the snares the world sets for us. Jesus said the healthy don't need a physician, but the sick, the con-fused, the victims of their own bad judgements and mistakes." She hesitated, gazing up at him honestly, but quite tenderly. "We all make mistakes."

Pilate stared straight ahead into the blackness, his clenched hands white on the wet wooden railing, and she went on: "He said his work was for the lost ones, to reclaim them. He said to seek his acceptance and you would find it, to forgive and you would be forgiven, and always to love and strengthen each other, no matter what. You're not really alone, Pilate."

He drew in a heavy breath of air, his muscles loosening from their military mold and the vitus staff slipped from his relaxing fingers and fell into the sea. "Is it possible?" She locked her arms around him, burying her face on his chest, and Pilate, stroking her hair, looked up at the range of stars flecking the night around them.

Tiberius died before Pilate could appear for the investigation, and fourth-century church historian Eusebius cites ancient reports that Pilate afterward fell into such calamities that he committed suicide. Other ancient traditions, however, say that he, like his wife, became a Christian and that for affirming it openly, he was beheaded in Rome and his body thrown in the river Tiber. Christian friends retrieved it and buried him in France where a hill near Vienne still bears his name.

To Eastern churches, both he and Procula are numbered among the saints of a faith that says its Lord whom Pilate crucified died in agonizing forgiveness and love for all the world's crucifiers of goodness who see their wrongdoing and their need for such mercy.

PART 5
The Sympathizers

1.
Nicodemus

The wind is against you, old man. Why fight it? Give in. Be sensible and heed the ruling pressure of the day. It's politics. It is approved. It bears the sanction of the ruling crowd and crown of Caesar's power and majesty. And yet, you bridle at this course! Despite the certain tide and temper of the times, you question, criticize and even think on furthering your dissent. What ails thee, Nicodemus, great old rabbi, learned teacher, sage of Israel?

How stubbornly you fret. "They drink the wine of violence!" So the prophets often warned in vain. Be realistic. It is fruitless to object. The thing is set, the order sealed and duly authorized. The man will die. "Oh God, thy justice is turned back, and truth is fallen in the public squares." You tread on dangerous ground, gray-bearded one, and few will stand beside you in this hour. You realize this full well. As a member of the Temple court, the Sanhedrin, you already have felt the lash of scorn for sympathizing with the rebel Galilean. That only brought an accusing taunt from your fellow councilors. "Are you from Galilee, too?"

Now the incriminating gale blows even stronger. And who could move against it, who resist? Even the apostles of Jesus, his closest companions, have scattered into hiding, silence, and fear. One, Judas, had sold him out, and another, Peter, disavowed him. None of the others raised a voice in protest, not a single word.

You have the most to lose. Your title, fortune, reputation. Why risk it all? How much safer and discreet to acquiesce, to nod agreeably and go along with the prevailing current. Yet you balk, Nicodemus. You sense another kind of wind that stirs the conscience and the soul. You remember that night, a year ago, when you talked with this Galilean and he spoke of that other wind.

It had been a puzzling interview and Nicodemus could not erase its effect on him. In his responsibility as an eminent instructor in the academies of Jerusalem, and one to whom others looked for guidance, he had visited Jesus privately to inquire into his unconventional teachings. Nicodemus had wanted to determine, fairly and open-mindedly, just why some of his colleagues were so disturbed by the ways of the newcomer from the north. After all, a midrash taught: "If an unrecognized prophet accomplishes some sign, he is to be listented to."

And many amazing signs had attended the work of this Jesus, attracting multitudes of the unschooled and common people of the land.

Nicodemus, seeking a fair understanding of the opposed man, had gone to see him privately by night, as related in the third chapter of the Book of John. He addressed the Nazarene as a fellow teacher. "Rabbi, we know that you are a teacher come from God; for no one can do these signs that you do unless God is with him." Jesus, dismissing the outward wonders, had said that what mattered chiefly was man's inner condition, that he must renounce his self-righteous pride, recognize his moral inadequacies and become dependent on God like a little child. "Truly, truly, I say to you, unless one is born anew, he cannot see the kingdom of God. . . . You must be born anew."

"How can a man be born when he is old?" Nicodemus asked. The mystical implications seemed quite impractical. "How can this be?" Jesus observed that even nature had its unseen realities, and much more the spiritual qualities. "The wind blows where it wills, and you hear the sound of it, but you do not know whence it comes or whither it goes; so it is with everyone who is born of the spirit."

Then he spoke even more puzzlingly of his being offered up, a light to the world, not to condemn it but to save it. "For God so loved the world that he gave his only son, that whosoever believes in him should not perish but have eternal life."

The wind blows, Nicodemus, both that inner breath, and the earthly tempest that would destroy this radical teacher from the hills. Many of you sensitive Pharisees were intrigued by him, but there appeared no chance to avert his doom.

When the decision was put before the Sanhedrin, meeting in the Chamber of Hewn Stone, adjoining Pilate's apartments at the Fortress Antonia, you had protested against prejudging the man without deliberation or evidence. "Does our law judge a man without first giving him a hearing and learning what he does?" you had complained indignantly. But that only drew abusive insinuations about your own loyalty to the government. Other Pharisees on the council, including the venerable Gamaliel and Joseph of Arimathea, also were tolerantly disposed toward the nonconformist Jesus, but only you, Nicodemus, dared to declare your dissent openly.

However, the die was cast and the Book of Nicodemus says the erudite old Nicodemus visited Pilate and begged him to spare Jesus. "He is a man who has

wrought many wonderful signs," Nicodemus pleaded.
"If the signs which he doeth are of God, they will
stand, but if they be of men, they will come to naught.
Let him go, and do him no harm."

It was useless. It did not slow the storm of death. It
only implicated you, old Nicodemus. Caiaphas, the
high priest confirmed in office by Pilate, accused you
of being a confederate of Christ and suggested you
cast your lot with him.

"Amen and amen," you whispered to yourself.

The Gospels record that you helped bury Jesus.
Other ancient manuscripts relate that you were de-
prived of office, banished from Jerusalem, baptized by
Peter and John, and later buried in a common grave
with Gamaliel and the first Christian martyr, Stephen.
You could have kept silent, Nicodemus. You could
have simply accepted the dominant current of the
time. It would have been more practical to comply, to
hold your tongue, when the world's wind blows strong.
But you didn't do that, Nicodemus (whose name means
"conqueror of the people"). You fought back. You
protested. You raised a lone voice for justice, mercy,
and honor. It cost you, Nicodemus.

It wasn't practical. Neither did that process which
Jesus expounded about being "born anew" sound practical. But there are other currents of life in this universe
besides the practical, utilitarian winds of the moment.
And you traveled with that other wind, Nicodemus, on
that eternally regenerating springtide of truth, which,
even when crushed, bursts forth anew. You did not
conquer the passing gusts, old conqueror, but you
mastered the weather of life.

"Amen," and "Amen."

2.
The Centurion

Through the last watches of the night he had paced the guardroom floor, sleepless, disgusted, as the wheels of oppression turned. Bitterly, he had heard the shifty procurator pass sentence. And now Pretonius marched the victims toward Golgotha, the Place of the Skulls.

Keep them moving. Don't think about the consequences. Follow orders and get it over with. Leave the rest to the imperial magistrates. It was not his affair. Or was it? "Stand back!" He lashed out at the pressing crowds with the vine-staff emblem of his military rank.

Up ahead, a trumpeter and herald moved at the front of the column, bearing the decree of execution. Behind them trudged the three prisoners, crossbeams on their shoulders, prodded along by the mantiple of soldiers that Pretonius had detailed for the assignment. It galled him fiercely, particularly in the case of that bloodily beaten but uncomplaining one called Jesus. The man had been buffeted about all night, and at Pilate's orders, viciously flogged with the lead-tipped *flagallum,* his back and arms mangled into gory pulps.

185

Yet, even as his flesh failed and his limbs faltered, there remained about him a firmness, a commanding nobility. Several times he fell under the heavy wooden *patibulum.*

"Take over that beam!" Pretonius snagged a bystander from the sidelines, a husky African, and put him to carrying the crosspiece. The dismal procession moved out again, crawling through the cramped Jerusalem streets. If he could only stop the entire grisly spectacle, turn the culprits loose, countermand the whole misbegotten business.

Pretonius muttered an oath, glancing about at the profusion of dark, gaping eyes, the sobbing native women pressing in close to the mauled prisoner, Jesus, who murmured something to them, gravely, sympathetically, concerned with them instead of himself. "Weep not for me. . ." So this was justice! Rome, the astute mistress, "goddess of the earth," guardian of the virtues, its will enforced by its legions.

If Pretonius had only been there, he would not have been given this present foul detail. Sweat slid down his face, and with the edge of his cape-like *sagum,* he wiped his eyes. Seething inwardly, outraged at what he was doing, yet he still headed toward it. He moved against his own convictions. He negated himself. He yielded to other dominating compulsions.

Duty, discipline, allegiance to the emperor. That was his controlling code. All his adult days he had lived by it. He was a centurion, a career officer, dependable, regular, a commander of one hundred men. Rome, not he, made his choices. He moved, not by his own standards, but by the sign of the Eagle. There was nothing he could do. The powers and dominions of the world had fixed the course, and all a man could do was follow it, accept it, adapt to it, get in step. He was a soldier, under orders. Even if he weren't you couldn't do much, if anything. One man couldn't stop it. The world didn't move these days by personal recti-

tude, by private evaluations; and perhaps never did
and never would.

Somewhere along the line, the authorities decided,
and the momentum gathered, and you hurtled along
with it. Even the authorities, confirming and echoing
one another, were thereby caught in it until no one
could ascertain definitely just where, why or how it
all began. Drowned in it was the conscience of the individual, which is the only place where conscience
resides. But should a man let that happen? Could he
do it and still be a man? And still really survive
himself?

Pretonius stared at the dusty cobblestones under-
foot, noting the red trail left there by the cartage of
some newly slaughtered animal. Then, nausea filling
his throat, he realized the blood came not from an
animal, but from that lacerated Jewish rabbi being
driven to execution.

The whole twisted business was a blatant sham, and
Pretonius knew it. He was part of the detachment that
arrested the man last night outside the walls, and
which had hustled him from place to place, trying to
determine just what tribunal would handle the pro-
ceedings against him. The titled local sycophants, who
worked with Rome, originally questioned him, and
their flunkies slapped him around, seeking in vain to
exact some damning statement from him. "I have
spoken openly to the world," he said. A rare policy,
in these conniving times. Like water in a torrent.

Even the man's trusted comrades deserted him,
spurned him, repudiated him. "I do not know the
man!" swore his chief apostle, Peter, cursing vehemently. "I do not know him!" The whole, rickety,
mass-moulded system had turned on its prey of the
moment, and joined in crushing him.

Step by step against the mounting sun, his grim
parade passed through the gate, and climbed the rocky
hill where the uprights stood. Revolted, angry, his eyes

red with fatigue and anguish, he carried out the world's
will. He hung Jesus until he was dead, and had him
speared in the side to make his deed final. But even as
he did so, his conscience rebelled and he flung its
lonely protest into the darkened sky. Both Matthew
and Luke record it. "Certainly this man was innocent,"
he cried.

Pretonius, the reliable soldier, the solid citizen. He
rejected his action even as he performed it. The Eagle
screamed, and the soldier functioned; his reflexes
worked and his sword flashed, obedient to men, driven
by overwhelming forces that seemed beyond personal
control. Yet that finer force in the individual, *in foro
conscientiae,* still pulsed, insisting on the right even
as he succumbed to the wrong, proclaiming truth, even
as it choked beneath the avalanche of the world's col-
lective depredations.

Pretonius sank to his knees, his face an ashen, corrugated mask, the dripping spear beside him. A dutiful
Roman, a responsible man, he had done his duty. But
he had violated his fundamental being. He had violated
himself. At the world's bidding, he was also impaled
on that far-spread cross. He, too, was its victim. He,
too, was sacrificed, and he shuddered.

"Truly, this *was* the son of God."

3.
The African

Like many another tourist, Simon saw the martial procession coming down the hill from the Fortress Antonia. Curious, he stopped to watch it. He could make out three prisoners, each carrying a heavy wooden beam.

It seemed strange— a hanging during the holiday week. Simon shrugged, worked the betel nut in his jaw, and spat. He was a giant of a man, dark of skin, with a proud, erect stance. His massive hands were callused and he had the sun-crinkled eyes of a farmer. But his turban and mantle were of the finest woven wool. He came from Cyrene, in Libya's fertile, coastal hills of Africa, where he and his sons, Rufus and Alexander, raised great fields of cotton. Marketing business may have brought him on this trip to Jerusalem.

From up the street, the formation approached slowly, led by a Roman herald bearing the decree of execution. Behind trudged the prisoners, prodded along by four soldiers. Others marched at the rear, their orange-colored capes rippling at their backs. A centurion moved at the side of the column, occasionally barking orders.

Simon found his attention riveted on one of the victims, a slender, bearded man, whose face was scratched, blood-streaked, and puffed with ashen bruises. His arms bore the jagged gashes of the metal and bone-tipped lash.

Neither of the other two men, both burly, vicious-looking ruffians, showed any signs of flogging. Only the one appeared gravely hurt and weakened. Red stains soaked the back of his robe. Yet with all of the marks of abuse and injury, there was about him a formidable strength. He was broken, crushed, but somehow, still relentlessly determined in his walk to death. Simon felt a surge of admiration.

The crowd had thickened, but when the big man from Africa stepped forward a bit, the others edged aside, opening a path. He had not intended to move closer, but the action came involuntarily. His ears picked up scatterings of talk now, and some of the onlookers pointed their fingers. "The Nazarene," they said. "The disturber, Jesus." The other two condemned men were said to be bandits, Dysmas and Gestas.

The hands of all three were tied, held aloft athwart the wooden beams which rested on their right shoulders. To Simon's practiced eye, the boards looked about four cubits (six feet) long, about two palms wide and three fingers thick. These were the horizontal pieces of the crosses on which they would die. The uprights already were in place on the hill, Calvary.

Simon's eyes narrowed as he watched the agonized progress of the Nazarene. The man's breath came in light, rapid gasps, and he tottered uncontrollably each time he advanced a foot.

Then, just as the prisoners came abreast of Simon, the Nazarene stumbled on a jutting cobblestone and pitched forward on the pavement. The board slammed against his back. A soldier cursed. Another one, muttering, slid the board free, and the centurion came running up to get the prisoner back on his feet. Once up, the officer surveyed the Nazarene dubiously and shook his head. Then his irritated gaze swept the crowd. Simon stood out, a natural physical specimen for a heavy load. The centurion jabbed a finger at him—"You!"

Simon eyed the soldier warily. He didn't like jumping to Roman commands. Then he glanced at the battered prisoner, and that puzzling attraction, another sort of command, rang in him. He stroked his hips and strolled over beside the crossbeam. With a quick, easy dip of powerful arms, he swung it to his shoulder. Then he turned and for the first time his eyes met those of Jesus.

It was only an instant, but to Simon it held an eternity of affection received. Those eyes, despite all the man's mistreatment, swam with a strangely rich animation, with a deep knowledge and immense love. There was something else, too, in the flash of a single look, he knew you utterly, through and through, and made you a cherished companion. There were no guarded reservations, no barriers in those eyes. Never before had Simon felt so fully wanted, so genuinely needed and approved. It wasn't so much the gratitude that he saw in that look, but a limitless understanding that smiled approval and kinship.

At a barked order, the procession resumed and Simon stepped along beside the prisoner, hardly aware of the weight on his shoulder. It seemed light, and he couldn't shake off a baffling sensation. He had an urge to thank this condemned man, Jesus, for the chance to carry the beam. It just didn't make sense.

Jesus walked more steadily now, and Simon heard him sigh with relief. It was about six furlongs (three-fourths of a mile) out to the hill of crucifixion, also called Golgotha.

No record tells what conversations passed between Simon and Jesus on that somber walk together, but it is possible that they spoke, that Jesus explained something of his lone, terrible mission to the world.

"I am the good shepherd. . . . I lay down my life for the sheep." A farmer like Simon would understand such language. "I lay down my life that I may take it again. . . . He who believes in me, though he die, yet shall he live again."

They reached the hill.

The prisoners were stripped and laid on their backs while their outstretched arms were nailed to the crossbeams. These were then hoisted by pulleys to the upright stakes, lashed in place, and the victims' feet nailed to the stakes.

Simon could help Jesus no more. The hours of torture began—the crawling, creeping, muscle-cramping, lung-constricting horror of crucifixion—the slow death of pain, the cruelest form of execution ever devised.

Loud were the taunts. Bitter the mockery. Jesus implored, "Father, forgive them. . . ." The soldiers gambled, and the crowd gawked. "My God, my God . . ." The sky turned black and the earth shook. "It is finished."

Slowly Simon turned and walked away. The big African would never be the same again. His strong arms had taken him into the embrace of stronger arms. "Take my yoke upon you, and learn from me." Jesus had said. "For my yoke is easy, and my burden is light."

In the years afterward, Simon from Cyrene labored with Jesus' apostles, as did his two sons Rufus and Alexander, whose names are mentioned in the Gospel of Mark, and whose later activity is cited in the Books of Acts and Romans. Simon had discovered, suddenly and without plan, that life's greatest compensation came when he took up a cross and followed Jesus.

4.
The Bandit

It was a stinking rock-heap, littered with bones and crawling with vermin and reptiles. As he reached the top, Dysmas eased the split log off his shoulder and let it tumble behind him, hoping it slammed against some *gedud*, those cursed Roman legionnaires.

They stripped the clothes off him and the other doomed men, then shoved the three flat on their backs and bound their outstretched arms to the timbers. Dysmas stared up narrowly at the helmeted, shaven faces bending over him, and above them, at the stationary upright posts thrusting into the sky.

So this was Golgotha, the "place of the skull." An unyielding hate smouldered in Dysmas' lidded eyes. The *ratsach*, the murderers! The heathen oppressors! Several of them held him down as they drove spikes through his wrists to secure his arms in place. His body jerked with each blow of the mallet. Then he lay quivering, vaguely hearing the howls from his outlaw crony, Gestas, as they nailed him to the wood. The third one didn't even whimper.

Dysmas knew it was going to be terrible, but he

didn't know how much so until they began tugging the rope pulleys, hauling him up the post, splinters knifing into his bare back, his impaled arms stretching to hold his insides together. At the top of the uprights, the crossbeams dropped into the notch with an excruciating jolt to his suspended weight. His shoulders snapped out of joint, clamping his ribs and the air whooshed out of him. The world went black. When he came to, vomit was raining into his beard and he was sucking part of it back with each gasp for breath. The soldiers had put his legs astraddle a peg in the post and nailed down his feet so he could push himself up slightly to grab a swallow of air.

The slow, tormenting death began.

A boiling sun rode above the Moab mountains to the east. It was the third hour, 9:00 A.M. On the three crosses, Jesus of Nazareth, the "friend of sinners" and companion of the lowly and the lost, hung between two of that same miserable lot, a pair of robbers.

Banditry and anti-Roman resistance were regarded synonymously in that period. Also, since crucifixion was reserved for slaves and insurrectionists, all three evidently were hung as rebels. In Jesus' case, this was specifically indicated on a Roman tag hung on his neck.

Ancient tradition identifies the two bandits as tough, violent Jews, plunderers of trade caravans, despoilers of the rich, guerrilla fighters against oppression who had turned to wanton pillage. Such underground turbulence was common during the Roman occupation.

Dysmas hung to the right of Jesus, Gestas on the left. Legend pictures Gestas as a barbarous highwayman who relished killing; while Dysmas, a one-time innkeeper, had turned to crime to ravage the ruling aliens and rob the wealthy to feed the ragged cave-dwellers.

Long before, it is related, the pair had encountered Joseph and Mary in their flight to Egypt with the infant Jesus, and Dysmas had bribed his brutal partner to let

the family alone. This story, recorded in ancient
apocryphal books, suggests the two were considerably
older than Jesus.

Now all three had met again, hanging side-by-side,
while ravens and vultures circled overhead. At choking
intervals, Dysmas heaved himself upward by pressure
on his pinioned feet in order to inhale. It was impossible while his torso sagged because the tautly stretched
chest tendons constricted the rib cage and kept the
lungs flat. But he couldn't hold himself up for long.
Muscular cramps twisted like knives through his body.
And each time, as he slumped downward again, de-
pleted, it stifled his breathing.

Already, the jagged nail wounds swelled into inflamed monstrosities at his wrists and feet, trickling
blood. But the large-headed spikes were strategically
placed to hold—placed behind the tough ligament
above the heel, and between the two large wrist tendons, rather than through the hands from which nails
gradually ripped out between the finger bones.

The onset of the traumatic fevers came soon, but in
his clearer moments, Dysmas could hear the jeers by
the soldiers and other governmental onlookers directed
at the young man dying beside him, Jesus. "Aha! He
saved others; he cannot save himself. He trusts in God;
let God deliver him now, for he said, 'I am the son
of God.' If he is the king of Israel; let him come down
from the cross, and we will believe him."

Turning his head slightly—it felt as huge and heavy
as a millstone—Dysmas looked blurrily at this final
companion, a pitifully forbearing fellow, a terrible
sadness in his eyes, but also a flaming tenderness, an
incredible loving submissiveness.

But he was failing fast, his body having been previously torn and mutilated by flogging. A convulsion
seized Dysmas and even as he fought through it, his
mind stormed with anger. The viles hosts of Edom!
The stonehearted Roman swine, flogging a man with-

out limit with their leaded scourges, often killing them that way! Even though Jewish subordinates had picked up the penalty, they restricted it to no more than thirty-nine lashes, with a non-leaded whip. But the foreigners laid on without any humane restraints.

"Father, forgive them; for they know not what they do."

The words of Jesus, the startling magnanimity, came bounding at Dysmas, breaking into his agony and anger, into the pounding ache in his head. He raised himself, panting, and sank again. His vision wavered and the blazing sun set off rings of fire and blackness that seemed to stream endlessly toward him, in his sight or else in his mind, fire and blackness, blackness and fire, and the massive thudding in his head. Again, voices reached him, this time the raging, begging, mocking fury of Gestas. "Are you not the Christ?" he railed. "Save yourself and us." The spleen and scorn of a trustless lifetime, panicked for some trick to avoid the consequences.

It went on, as the old, non-canonical accounts have it. "Why callest thou thyself son of God and canst not help thyself? I behold thee, not as a man, but as a wild beast caught and perishing along with me."

Dysmas, in that extremity, suddenly saw something more. The onrushing rings of pain whirling at Dysmas took on other images, and straining, blinking, he turned his head and gasped, "I know thee Christ . . . the son of God. I see thee, Christ worshiped by ten thousand times ten thousand . . . forgive my sins."

Breath failed him, the bands like iron clamping his chest again, and he forced himself up, shaking violently, but the air was somehow more blessed, and he looked down regretfully at his hard old cohort, Gestas. "Do you not fear God? Not even now, as we die under the same sentence of condemnation? And we indeed justly for . . . our deeds; but this man has done nothing wrong."

Winded, his voice trailed into a thin, sobbing cry.

"Jesus, remember me when you come in your kingly power." It was a prayer struggling out of the emptiness of a lifetime, but which could still find trust amid its terrors.

And Jesus said, "Truly, I say to you, today you will be with me in paradise."

A strange wave of relief washed over Dysmas, muting the assaults of the sun, the cramping of muscles, the bursting surcharge of blood in his arteries and head. The Roman centurion put a sponge soaked in myrrhed wine on the end of a javelin and held it up to Jesus, a potion to deaden pain. It touched Jesus' lips but he turned his face aside.

Dysmas watched, puzzled at his new reactions, but not confused, even though the confusion kept coming and going, but not now, and he, too, the forgiven, now could forgive and love—love even the foreign executioners. Tears ran down his cheeks among the insects crawling there.

It was the sixth hour, noon; the sky darkened and tremors shook the earth. The eclipse lasted until the ninth hour (3:00 P.M.). Although crucifixion normally took two or three days, the legionnaires were under orders to conclude it before nightfall because of the Passover festival.

They broke the legs of the two thieves so they could no longer lift their bodies, thus bringing on speedy asphyxia. Jesus, weakened by the earlier flogging, was already dead. So his legs were not broken. But as a finishing stroke, a soldier ran a spear into his side, which drained water and blood, indicating he died of a ruptured heart.

So ended the worldly career of Jesus, friend of the underdog, advocate of the outcasts, healer of lepers, champion of the despised, the illiterate and lawless sinners, confederate in death as in life of the same lowly company—the least, last, and lost. The man who said he had come to "set at liberty those who are oppressed" was with them to the end, doing that work, opening new gates to the captives. And in his direst moment, it was one of them, a thief, who saw and accepted that saving opportunity, while respectable society turned its back.

5.
Joseph of Arimathea

Shades of disgrace trailed him. Reproachful eyes peered from behind the hedges, and tongues of slander whispered against him as they did against the prophets of old. Denounce him! Let us denonce him!" Joseph of Arimathea walked a treacherous path. It had led him into conflict with his class, into challenging his own judicial order, into defense of a convicted capital offender and at last, into claiming the man's body from the Romans who condemned him.

Joseph, the warmhearted and eloquent country rabbi who had risen to distinction in the leading institutions of the holy city, followed a road that could bring him to ruin. It descended into the dark desert of the cross. But for him, there was no turning back. "Like a weaver, I have rolled up my life." Let the owls watch, and the jackals circle around, he had determined on a final gesture of respect to the dead Galilean, however inexpedient.

"Give me this stranger," he had requested of Pontius Pilate in a bold and direct confrontation, a scene noted in Scripture and detailed in other early writings. After each round of argument, Joseph had repeated his insistent plea, "Give me this stranger." Pilate, disturbed and dubious at first, had warned that it seemed provocative and ill-advised in this messy case. Finally, however, after summoning the centurion in charge of the execution to verify that Jesus was dead, the governor had testily consented, "Take him!"

So now the audacious rabbi from Arimathea, a tiny mountain village near the Samaritan border, hastened to provide an honorable burial for the crucified rabbi from another rural hamlet, Nazareth. None of the slain man's comrades or relatives had dared intervene to perform that service. Mostly they had disappeared, scattered in fright. But Joseph, a virtual outsider, a prominent public figure, a respected member of the Sanhedrin who had not consented to the charges against Jesus, and who courageously clung to his position, even after it was spurned, stepped forward to attend the fallen, unwanted one, whom others had abandoned or shunned.

A nervy man, this Arimathean, this son of the up-country. His vigor and incisive intelligence had earned him ranking prestige in the sophsticated circles of Jerusalem after he moved there from his native town. He also had prospered, and owned a spacious house and grounds. He would not lightly jeopardize this estate. Yet now he approached an incriminating task. Under precepts of the Torah, it was defiling to touch the corpse of a condemned man, especially one crucified. "A hanged man is accursed," Moses wrote. In Israel, such death was the utmost infamy and shame.

No executed criminal, however he dies, would be laid in a family tomb, much less a crucified one. Yet Joseph so intended, in the face of the ostracism this likely would cause him.

He hurried, for the sun declined. From the praetorium, he crossed the Sextus bridge to the upper city, and at his house bade his servants accompany him, taking along a flat cypress litter. He led them out of the Fish gate and up the rocky hill beyond the city walls and to the foot of the sapless tree where Jesus hung. There, Nicodemus, another Pharisee on the Sanhedrin who had wanted Jesus spared, joined Joseph in extracting the nails and lowering the bruised and lifeless body from the scaffold to the ground.

Two other bodies hung there. The Roman constabulary, in most occupied territories, left the dead exposed on the crosses to be devoured by carrion birds and hyenas. But in Israel, the bodies were taken down and dumped into a handy pit because of the Judaic injunction that bodies left hanging would pollute the land. The soldiers, tradition relates, tossed the corpses of the two thieves into an abandoned cistern used for garbage.

But the body of Jesus was borne by Joseph, Nicodemus, and their servants to the peaceful, landscaped "Garden of Joseph," where fountains splashed, flowers grew, and where a newly hewn tomb opened in the face of a stone embankment. It was the twelfth hour (6:00 P.M.), and nighthawks called in the twilight.

No weeping clan accompanied that departed son there. No professional mourners led the procession, as was customary in Jewish funerals. No sad flutes played; no kinsmen sobbed, "Alas, alas!" No wailing women rent their garments and threw dust in their hair. It was a lonely, desolate affair. From a distance, only two friends of Jesus — both women — watched silently through the trees as the two kindly rabbis rendered the last offices for the abased and forsaken Galilean.

Joseph had prepared a new tomb for himself and his family. Now it would become the resting place for the stranger. While still outside in the waning light, the men washed the body and anointed it with aromatic nard. They closed the eyelids, bound up the jaws, and swathed the hands and feet with linen strips, binding them together. Between the folds of cloth, they spread a mixture of myrrh and aloes to retard decomposition. However, Judaism did not practice embalming, nor use coffins. An outer shroud was wrapped around the body before it was carried into the sepulchre.

Inside it was placed on one of several recessed ledges, hewn into the side walls. Nicodemus had brought one hundred pounds of fragrant ointments, and the unused portion was left beside the body, perfuming the air of that dark, cool chamber. "Make ready a place for this righteous man." The ancient Jewish prayer may have been on Joseph's lips. "We bless thee, O Eternal God, who restoreth the soul."

He and the others withdrew. The Roman guard, assigned by Pilate, rolled the huge disk-shaped stone along its groove until it covered the mouth of the tomb, and sealed it with metal straps.

The task was done.

Joseph, out of some dauntless urging of mind and character, had befriended the friendless, even in death. Although publicly never associated with Jesus before, his actions indicate he had developed some secret regard for the upsetting teacher from the north. Perhaps the similar rural origins—and the difficulties Jesus had encountered in the city—struck some responsive chord in Joseph. Perhaps, among the colonnades of the Temple, Joseph had overheard him speaking, and his heart had leaped within him.

Unlike the dominant, but soon-repudiated Sadducean party, Joseph believed in the immortality of the soul, in the enduring rabbinic tradition of the Pharisees. As Scripture notes, he held the messianic hope for the kingdom of God, confident that the Lord acts in human history. Whatever his reasons, Joseph took his stand with a defamed and marked man, not counting the costs, realizing that it would arouse resentment in high quarters. By his decision, he himself became a marked man.

Tradition recounts that on the second day after the burial, an angry group accosted him, threatening to throw him into the same well with the two thieves. Instead, he was imprisoned. But he later escaped. According to legend, he became a wandering Christian disciple, carrying with him the cup which Christ used at his last supper. He is said to have transported the faith to the British Isles, where, spent by his labors, he sighed, "We be weary all," thereby giving the name to England's Wirral Hill.

The country rabbi from Arimathea traveled a rare and precarious road. It led him through forbidding doors, among offended colleagues through disapproving suburbs. It led him to a hill where thunder rattled in the afternoon and into a garden of drooping willows where a stone door closed, and it was night.

"It is good to be here," he said, heedless of the consequences. "I am content."

6.
The Sergeant

It grew chilly as the night wore on. The Roman sergeant tossed more sticks on the campfire and stood warming his hands. Another soldier sat cross-legged, a sheepskin over his shoulders, munching a slab of cheese. Their spears leaned against a square-shaped tent, pitched in a private grove outside Jerusalem where the crucified Nazarene had been entombed. With the toe of his boot, the sergeant listlessly nudged some scattered coals back into the fire. He yawned and stretched his arms. In an isolated spot like this, guard duty was particularly monotonous.

The watch had been maintained since late on the sixth day of the week. With the provincial Sabbath over at sunset, it now was near midnight in the new week's first day. To begin with, there had been quite a stir about the assignment. The sergeant had been on post at the procurator's quarters when the Sadducean priests came to Pilate about it.

"Sir," they fretted, "we remember how that impostor said while he was still alive, 'After three days I will rise again.' Therefore, order the sepulchre made secure until the third day."

As the worried politicians put it, the Nazarene's followers might come and steal his body and then spread reports that he had risen from the dead. "The last fraud will be worse than the first," the priests insisted. "Go make it as secure as you can," Pilate consented peevishly, as related in ancient non-biblical literature.

For the first night, and through most of the sabbath, he supplied nearly an entire platoon—thirty men under a centurion. About a thousand people, mostly idlers, had wandered out to the tomb on the second day after the crucifixion to stare and make jests. But by late afternoon, the place was deserted and with public curiosity waning, the guard had been reduced to a regular two-man detail.

The sergeant pulled his hooded *pacnula* closer about his neck and slumped against a tree. What a weird business this was—guarding a corpse! He glanced at the face of the tomb. It was dug into a fourteen-foot bluff, gray, and cold-looking in the gloom. A huge circular stone, about five feet in diameter, completely covered the opening. With great hoisting and heaving, it had been rolled into a groove cut at the base of the opening, and sealed there with seven pegs. Before the sealing, the sergeant had watched the two rich Jewish notables, Nicodemus and Joseph of Arimathea, wrapping the body in linens rubbed with gummy, brown myrrh and aloes.

To the sergeant, the extraordinary activity about the case—all this ado over a dead man—seemed ridiculous, And that babble about being raised to life again! Great Caesar's ghost! He picked up a stone and flung it at the face of the tomb. It banged against the rock wall and clattered down into the blackness of the ground.

Then, suddenly, without a moment's notice, everything became quiet. Silence.

He felt an obscure uneasiness. He thought of moving about, scuffling his feet to break the spell, but stood as if rooted. All life seemed momentarily suspended, halted, pausing on the verge of . . . he knew not what. The stars shone brightly, though. In fact, they seemed brighter than before. They were brighter. They were a great deal brighter. What was happening? What was wrong with his eyes? That light . . . that light in the sky!

It appeared as if a fissure was forming on the roof of the world, with a white brilliance pouring through a celestial door opening. Its blinding purity flashed downward, shimmering, cascading in a single, pinpoint arrow of light. The sergeant flung his arms over his eyes, a strangled cry at his throat. A shattering blast rent his eardrums, although he had an odd feeling that there really was no sound at all, as if the lightning had burst in his own head. A violent shaking seized the earth, or else simply him, and he felt himself falling. There was another thunderous roar, a laughing roar, like a whole army shouting a triumph.

He had no sensation at all of hitting the ground, but he realized he was there, flat on his belly, his face twisted to one side in the dirt, his eyes registering the gaping mouth of the tomb. The place shone like some huge, dazzling gem. The outlines of two figures took shape, like men but not like men, radiant, glowing heights of energy, and another appeared between them, taller, more resplendent still.

Then he could see no more. He didn't know how long he lay there. An instant, an hour . . . or had he lain there at all? All he knew was that suddenly he found himself standing again, his arms still folded at his chest, staring blankly into the flickering flames of the campfire. Everything was just as it had been before, as if he had imagined the whole thing. Except . . . he shook his head dazedly. Over there in a garden path stood some women and a man, or someone, talking to them, and the sergeant heard what sounded like, "Be not afraid."

He rubbed his chin shakily. These people—just some more inquisitive townsfolk. He must have dozed, had a wild dream, and they came up while he was having the feverish illusions. His whole body was in a cold sweat. Distrusting his senses, he turned slowly and looked at his companion. The soldier still sat there wrapped in his sheepskin. "Did you . . . ?" The soldier sat immobile as a dead man—his face waxen white.

Fearfully then, the sergeant raised his head and looked at the tomb. With a cry, he bolted. And so it happened that in the gray dawn of that long-ago morning, there were two soldiers racing, indeed, they seemed flying, out of the grove of Joseph of Arimathea and along the road to Jerusalem.

When they had calmed sufficiently to be coherent, they told their story to their superiors, including Pilate, and also the ruling Sadducees who paid them a large sum to conceal it and to claim that they had dozed and that the Nazarene's apostles must have stolen his body. The guard's flight into Jerusalem is noted in the last chapter of the Book of Matthew, as are the instructions given the soldiers. "Tell the people, 'His disciples came by night and stole him away while we were sleeping.' "

To fall asleep on guard duty was a capital offense, but Pilate and the Sadducees had to ignore this technicality to protect the tranquility of the state, namely, their own authority. The soldiers, if they valued their necks, dared not talk in public. But there was this conversation related in the ancient Gospel of Nicodemus between the Sadducean priests and the sergeant: "We were very much afraid and lay like dead men," he said haltingly. "Afterward, we heard the voice of the angel saying to the women at the tomb, 'Be not afraid.' "

The priests demanded: "To what women did he speak?"

The sergeant: "We do not know who they were."

The priests: "At what time was this?"

The sergeant: "At midnight."

The priests: "And wherefore did you not lay hold on them?"

The sergeant: "We were like dead men from fear, not expecting to see the light of day again, how could we lay hold on them?"

The priests: "As the Lord liveth, we do not believe you."

The sergeant: "Assuredly you have done well to swear that the Lord liveth, for indeed he does." The sergeant paused, his expression stubborn. He added quietly: "And Jesus is risen."

7.
The Women

In a man's world, the women stood firm. Strong, forthright men flinched and fled, but the women held fast. In the male-dominated society which struck Jesus down, most of his close friends left him—except for the women. They never gave up, even though the masculine corps of disciples collapsed in panic and despair.

It was strange, as puzzling as the legendary mystique attached to womanhood itself. And it carries an elemental rebuke to the disabilities which civilization, including the church, has habitually imposed on that allegedly frail, secondary creature fashioned of Adam's rib. Quickly, steadily, throughout the apparent calamity which befell the cause of Jesus, the women hung on, refusing to retreat. They confronted the storm from which their reputed superiors recoiled. In seeming disaster, they clung to hope.

Their role forms a muted but consistent pattern at nearly every juncture of the events, although some of it often goes unnoticed because of the scantiness of references to it, in keeping with the subsidiary status accorded women. Nevertheless, sprinkled through the Gospel accounts are the passing allusions—the swift, vivid cameos—disclosing the undaunted devotion of the women in the face of Jesus's midnight ordeal.

They, not his disciples, grieved with him along the *Via Dolorosa,* the Way of the Cross.

They, and only one other disciple, were present when he died.

They, but no apostles, followed him to the grave.

And they, not the disciples, carried the first glad tidings of his victory. "He is risen!" The women, in their unshaken trust and sensitivity of vision, discovered crowning triumph, while the pragmatic men cowered in despondency and doubt.

Not only was it the women among his followers who stuck by him during his abuse and death, but there also were other women, without any particular connection with him, who emerged in the midst of the fury to sympathize and plead for gentleness and mercy.

Another brief but poignant sidelight, noted only by Luke, reveals the wave of distressed, commiserating women who surged around Jesus on his way to crucifixion. "Daughters of Jerusalem, do not weep for me, but for yourselves and for your children," he said, his concern even then concentrated on others. In a crucifying world, he added prophetically, goodness faces hard struggle and suffering. "For if they do this when the wood is green, what will happen when it is dry?"

Besides the general compassionate outpouring of Jerusalem's women along that bleak route, tradition enumerates several intimate women believers who were in the sobbing throng, including Jesus' heartbroken mother, Mary. Another named is Veronica, who reportedly pushed forward to wipe his blood-streaked face with her veil. From then on to the end, and beyond, the women were close at hand. But the stalwart men? They were missing, gone, routed. The "pillars" had tumbled. Even the "rock," Peter, had slunk away, denying he knew Jesus. But the women persisted.

In that era, and to varying degrees since then, the
human race has allotted women a generally subordinate
part, classifying them as partly unqualified for the
masterful affairs of men. This was especially the case
in the environment which Jesus prodded, ruffled, and
shook. His disciples once stood aghast when he engaged in conversation with a strange Samaritan woman
at a well. A man wasn't supposed to condescend to talk
with a woman in public—even to his own wife.

The wife belonged in the house, subject to her husband's will. He could divorce her, by merely denouncing her as unfit. But not she him. She stood and served,
while the men dined; she did not sit with them. Her
oath was worthless in court and her husband could
refuse to honor any contract she signed. With rare ex-
ceptions, a daughter did not inherit from the father
—only the sons. Men thanked God daily that they
were not born women.

Outside Judaism, women were rated even lower. In
pagan Rome and Greece, female babies often were
exposed to die. If kept, they might be sold into slavery
to meet debts, or put to work as prostitutes.

Aristotle regarded women as inferior beings, midway
between freemen and slaves. In Rome, more considera-
tion was given courtesans than wives.

More than any other ancient society, Judaism
esteemed womanhood. The Mosaic commandments
required that mother, as well as father, be honored.
Furthermore, she was not a mere menial in the home,
but held a respected position, shown in the long line
of influential biblical women, Abraham's wife, Sarah;
Isaac's wife, Rebekah, the beautiful Rachel, Deborah,
Hanna, Hulday, counselor of high priest and king;
Solomon's mother, Bathsheba, even the merciless
Jezebel.

Nevertheless, women were regarded as less than
men, as an adjunct, a helpmate, not an equal. Men
ruled over them. A father contracted his daughter's

marriage and got a price for relinquishing his authority over her.

But this changed with the coming of Christ. His mother, Mary, exulting about it, offered a keenly discerning insight: "He has exalted them of low estate." In him, there was "neither Jew nor Greek," neither "male nor female," but all equally one. And in the culminating crisis of his life, it was those of "low estate," the women, who remained steadfastly bound to him with a love that overcame fear.

They were there at the cross: Mary Magdalene, whom Jesus had plucked from a wasted existence; his mother, Mary, and her sister, Salome, whose two tempestuous sons, James and John, were among the disciples.

Only one of those twelve, John, showed up on that devastating afternoon, but many women were there, those "who had followed Jesus from Galilee, ministering to him." Desperate, heartsick, yet still standing by him, still hoping in the midst of the hopelessness which had shattered the men.

They stood watching tearfully and devotedly as Jesus was taken down from the cross and carried on an open litter to the burial garden, still loving and believing with a passion that did not end with death.

They were there as the body was anointed, wrapped and laid in the tomb. None of the male companions appeared, only the women.

On the third day after Jesus' death, while the disciples still stayed in hiding, the women returned to the tomb, driven by a faith and intuition surer than any logic. Salome, Joanna, Mary, the mother of Jesus, and again, Mary Magdalene, found the tomb empty and a radiant messenger saying that Jesus "is not here; for he has risen. . . . Go quickly and tell his disciples."

Stunned and wildly elated, they ran back to the men's hideaway, pouring out the news. But the men scoffed. "An idle tale," they said, "and did not believe them."

Finally, however, the women persuaded Peter and John to return with them to the tomb. The men found it bafflingly empty, the face wrappings still there as if the body had dematerialized within it. Yet they made nothing of it and went away, still downcast and dubious.

But Mary Magdalene, that valorous soul, remained there in the garden, puzzling, yearning, crying. "Woman, why are you weeping?" Not looking up, her veil half covering her face, she thought the question came from the gardener.

But then he spoke again. "Mary."

And she knew. "Rabboni!"

Mary Magdalene, one who had been possessed of seven devils and had lived in debased melancholy until Jesus reclaimed her, raced to inform the men of his glory—his resurrection.

"I have seen the Lord!"

Later, in that mystically changed, yet intimately identifiable form, Jesus appeared to the men, reassuring and convincing them, turning that dispirited, frightened huddle at last into sturdy advocates of Christ.

But it was the women who set the standard. It was those supposedly timorous and frail ones, who demonstrated unwavering fortitude and devotion when the going was dark and dangerous, and who first carried that good news.

Although denied many places in his church in the years afterward, they showed their commitment to him when it was hard to do. In suffering and degradation, they honored him, and so they shared the first sunrise of his triumph. In that immemorial, world-shaking struggle from which the men drew back, the women enlisted unhesitatingly in its heroism and its eternal dominion.

PART 6
The Waiting and
the Wind

1.
Encounter on a Road

Two men strode along the road winding across the ridge northwest out of Jerusalem. Their dark faces bore the stamp of despair. "My hope is pulled up like a tree," said the older one, Cleopas. "They dashed him to pieces!" Grief, rage and shame mingled in his voice. "My soul is poured out within me. My eyes see no good."

The younger man, Simon, tightened the grip on his father's trembling hand, but still stared stonily ahead toward the reddening western horizon. "Alas, we are plunged into the pit. His house did not stand."

It was about thirty-five Roman stadia (four miles) to the town of Emmaus. Even though it had a century of about 100 legionnaires garrisoned there, it would be safer than Jerusalem, feverish with fears, tale-bearing, incendiary plots, and arrests. The whole country, from the uplands of rustic, defiant Galilee to the southern deserts of occupied Judea, smouldered with unrest and sparks of revolt against the alien, pagan oppressor.

The procurator's spies and mercenary swordsmen in

their breastplates and spiked boots roved the market-places. Zealots gathered stolen arms in their cellars and Roman cavalry trooped the countryside to hunt down unruly bands and burn their camps. But along the rocky road to Emmaus, in the lull of declining day, the two desolate footmen moved in a landscape of stillness.

It was the 17th of the spring month of Nisan, and only two days before, on the eve of the Sabbath, their adored and commanding champion, Jesus of Nazareth, had been crucified along with two insurgent brigands. He, too, had been branded a would-be insurrectionist. Pontius Pilate charged he had sought to recapture the national throne, as "King of the Jews."

"Bazah!" Cleopas lamented. "Vile, vile!" He spat and moisture caught in his untrimmed whiskers. "With wrath and deceit, they provoked their vassals to this iniquity. Yet his might prevailed not against them. Woe of woes!"

Sand flies swarmed up intermittently in the twilight air in front of them. The younger man sorrowed, "Howbeit, he went by his own feet into their snare?"

"Nay, that could not be—speak thus not!" Cleopas began but then he hesitated, recalling puzzling things which Jesus had foretold to the apostles many weeks ago around a campfire in Galilee. The words had been thrust aside then as meaningless, but now, stabbingly, they came back. "Behold, we are going up to Jerusalem, and everything that is written of the son of man by the prophets will be accomplished. For he will be delivered to the gentiles, and . . . they will scourge him and kill him . . ."

What had it meant? On what account? To what end? For now, nothing remained. Deliverance had not come. Forgiving, healing goodness had failed. Hope had perished. The two men proceeded along the road, questioning and grieving.

Cleopas and Simon had been among the seventy

disciples sent out two-by-two as yokefellows to spread Jesus' help to the lowly and rejected. A sister of Jesus' mother, Mary, was Cleopas' wife. She was among the women who watched at the crucifixion. She and Cleopas also had other sons. Two of them, Levi, known as Matthew, and stubby James the Less were among the twelve chief adjutants of Jesus. All in fear had deserted him at his arrest.

The apostles remained in hiding at the Jerusalem house of the widow Mary bath-Nabas. But others, to avoid arousing suspicion by their numbers, had dispersed, Cleopas and Simon among them. Utter stupefaction had prevailed there that morning, especially after the women brought their wild report of the empty tomb, and their visionary claims that Jesus had arisen. "An idle tale," the apostles had reproached.

Surely the strain and shock had caused these hallucinations, Cleopas reasoned. In like agitation, two apostles, Peter and John, had dashed recklessly out to the tomb. Dark and vacant, they found it. That made it even more dismaying. How witless to think on it. The cause had collapsed, the promises had sunk into the opprobrium of a criminal execution. A horrid finish! No strategems or fantasies could change it.

Yet dimly, disturbingly, another phrase spoken by Jesus returned in memory. ". . . and on the third day, he shall rise . . ." Cleopas jerked at the thong, tightening the girdle about his mantle, and tramped on. From somewhere, possibly from behind them, a wayfaring stranger had moved up beside them, intruding into their conversation, asking what troubled them so greatly as they walked.

The two men halted, staring glumly at the stranger. Cleopas sighed and said skeptically, "Are you the only visitor to Jerusalem who does not know the things that have happened there in these days?"

"What things?"

Cleopas shook his head and resumed the journey.

He recounted tersely the recent events and added bitterly, "We had hoped that he was the one to redeem
Israel."

A silence fell momentarily among them. Somewhat
annoyingly, the stranger stayed alongside. Then, in a
low voice, almost as if to himself, he said, "O foolish
men, and slow of heart to believe . . ." Without pausing, he went on in a kind of knowing, passionately
certain soliloquy, reviewing humanity's long, erratic
quest for devine companionship, his gnawing guilts,
the prophecies, the longings. It was a chasm to be
crossed in human life, as the stranger interpreted it,
or by one wholly identified with that life. As the
stranger spoke, Cleopas at first resented the man's
presumptions, but shortly, old prophecies and for-
gotten intimations began to stir in him in a new way.
"Behold, my servant . . . despised and rejected by men
. . ." Isaiah had written. ". . . bruised for our iniquities
. . . with his stripes we are healed."

And Jesus had spoken similarly. "Blessed are those
who mourn . . . those who are persecuted for righteousness sake . . . I am the way . . . the door . . . I go away,
and I will come to you . . . You will weep and lament
. . . But be of good cheer, I have overcome the world."

Distance and time passed, and all at once, Cleopas
realized they had reached the edge of Emmaus. It was
nearly dark, but the stranger appeared to be going on.
Cleopas urged, "Stay with us . . . The day is far spent."
They found a hostel, and sat down to a meal of bread,
cheese, and wine. The stranger took the bread, thank-
ing God for bringing forth sustenance from the earth,
broke it and gave it to them to eat.

Suddenly, in the common act, in sharing with the
stranger in the natural means through which mankind
exists, feels, thinks, and functions, Cleopas and his
son realized who he was. Then just as quickly, once
they knew, the sensory sight of him was gone.

The Book of Luke records: "And their eyes were

opened and they recognized him; and he vanished out of their sight." In a simple meal, they had found their Lord's presence.

Partaking of one, common bread, they had realized they were not left isolated and alone but that they drew their very blood from a universal substance from which all human life derives and in which he had become ineradicably involved. Amazed, Cleopas exclaimed, "Did not our hearts burn within us?" Simon agreed, a warm consolation surging in his veins.

They departed, in that same hour, to return to Jerusalem to tell the others. Utter dejection gripped those others. They dwelt in the opaque eye of death. Yet in that harsh darkness, a new clarity would come, so mighty that it would hurl those same men into the thick of danger, prisons, and martyrdom in order to proclaim it.

And after the slaying of one of them, Jesus' brother, James, his successor as bishop of Jerusalem would be Cleopas, the man of the road who first realized that the Lord still walks at man's side and communes in ordinary things, as simple as a piece of bread.

2.
The Uncertain Interlude

Toward evening they gathered in a large private house in the westerly Upper City of Jerusalem. They came singly and in little groups, slipping cautiously into the walled courtyard. They came listening, watching, afraid. The way of Jesus had become a dim, vertiginous passage.

A great hulk of a man, Simon Peter, sat at the foot of an outside stone stairway, his weather-toughened gaze registering each new arrival. They were desperate men, every one, but they also were the stout-hearted. It took that for them to be there. None knew what hostile eyes espied their coming, what tribunals judged. "... They will deliver you up ... they will scourge you ... kill you ... for my name's sake." Still they came, the remnant of the crucified.

The husky fisherman dragged a hand roughly across his face. "Oh Lord . . ." Their very lives seemed locked in a void, flung adrift in a formidable calm. "Oh Lord, be not far off." They could not alone find their way on that untraveled water. He sat there for a moment, his shaggy head bent. It might have been a mistake to summon them here, yet the need to take some action, to do something, anything, had driven in on him like a cloud.

Seven weeks had elapsed since the Master died.

Events during that period had alternately shocked, thrilled, and staggered his followers. At least eight times, the risen Jesus had been seen by individuals or groups, in a garden, by Cleopas and Simon on a road, by the apostles in a bolted room, on a mountaintop, by a few, by many, once by 500 simultaneously.

Yet always, he seemed changed, transformed, and appeared only for a short time. In between those astounding episodes, his adherents waited, questioned, fretted. Some gave up, drifted back to old pursuits. At one point, Peter himself had gone back to resume his fishing trade in Galilee, only to be confronted on a misty morning shore by Jesus, and a solemn charge: "Feed my sheep!" The apostle had returned to Jerusalem to do it.

But a sense of helplessness lay heavy on them all. The days dragged on. Now, out at the foregate of the house in Jerusalem, Matthew and Nathanael stood watch, welcoming the companions with a kiss of peace. Sighing, Peter got to his feet. To the west, above the wall, the last streaks of sun slid away.

The air held a pungent scent of wet lime, emanating from the whitewash freshly applied to the house before the Feast of the Weeks tomorrow, called Shabout or Pentecost. He glanced about austerely. The widow Mary bath-Nabas owned this spacious abode, a house of the rich. It was an unaccustomed place for these barefoot plowmen, these lean Galilean herdsmen and drovers. Strange that they should be here. Yet little else seemed familiar anymore. Wandering among them, embracing them, Peter could hear sporadically their muffled pleas, "Maranatha . . . Our Lord come."

Peter shook his head dourly. They might wait a long while before they saw the Lord again. "It is not for you to know the times or the seasons," the resurrected Jesus had said. Yet they still looked for him to return at once, banishing the Roman intruder and assuming earthly government.

Up to the end, just before he left them for the last time there on the mountain, they still insisted, "Lord will you at this time restore the kingdom to Israel?" Rejecting the purpose, he nonetheless said: "But you shall receive power when the Holy Spirit has come upon you; and you shall be my witnesses . . . to the end of the earth."

How? Wherewith? They were but a few wretched clods in this trampled corner of the continent. At first, his momentary reappearances had refired their strength. But they didn't retain it or build on it. So subtly it eluded them. They could cleave to him so long as he stayed within their sensory realm. But how hard, in that realm, to keep near him in another. So the lassitude had set in, the heaviness and the trepidations.

It had been forty-nine days since he rose. Nine days had passed since his last farewell on the mountain. The apostles since had dwelt in the large upper room of the widow's house closeted from roving vigilantes. Kinsmen of Jesus, his mother and other close consorts also had taken refuge there. They and the apostles had prayed diligently, in one accord, but without apparent effect.

They had found no recourse, no way out of their own uncertainties. Peter rubbed a fist to his chin. They had held back too long. They had to take some step, even the wrong one. By whispered friend-to-friend message, he had summoned the persevering ones here this night. Roving about the lamplit courtyard, Peter counted 120. Only these remained of the multitudes that once had rallied to Jesus. And questions lined their brows. Fear pinched their voices. "What news hast thou? Neighbors set forward our calamity."

To be sure there was cause for uneasiness. The land seethed with clandestine societies, some fanatically violent, and Caesar's militia and the collaborationist Sadducean hierarchy combined to crush these dissident movements.

Peter sent the widow's young son, John Mark, to fetch Matthew and Nathanael from the gate for the business at hand. In the distance, cries of the Roman guard posted for the night's first watch threaded along the city wall. He mounted the outside stair to the first landing. A slitted earthen lantern hung there, insects swirling about it. He stood in its glow, a massive figure with grizzled countenance, facing the 120 who still professed the Name. His chin jutted.

"Brethren," Peter began. They shuffled closer, their dark upturned faces converging below him. They might well be disappointed at his purpose. It could do little to dispel their shrinking inertia.

"Brethren, the Scripture had to be fulfilled . . . concerning Judas who was guide to those who arrested Jesus . . . It is written in the Book of Psalms, 'Let his habitation become desolate, and his office let another take.' "

"So be it," a voice called out. "Amen."

The betrayer, Judas Iscariot, guilt stricken by his deed, had hanged himself, and after his shunned body burst, it was buried in potter's field. Refilling the ranks of twelve would be a mere organizational matter. But it was something, better than standing still. Peter gazed about the shadowy crowd, waiting for a name to be put forward. It had to be someone from among the seventy Jesus had chosen personally to share his ministry.

"Joseph!" a voice rang out. "Joseph surnamed Justus!"

Peter nodded. Matthew took his stylus and scratched the name on a clay fragment and dropped it into a beaker. After a time, another candidate was called out. "Matthias, the gift of Jehovah." A second potsherd, inscribed with the new name, was dropped into the beaker. Peter took the vessel. The whole company joined in prayer. "Lord, who knowest the hearts of all men, show which one of these two thou hast chosen..."

Peter dropped to one knee, jogging the beaker up and down until one ostrakon jounced out of it. He picked it up, squinting at the letter. "Matthias, the gift of Jehovah," he announced. Once more, the Apostles were twelve. Somehow, by that step, Peter felt that the hard, dreary waiting had dissolved into a new stage. They had made a decision. They had done something, however slight. They had begun to act.

The sensation stayed with Peter as the night wore on and the meeting dispersed. The other apostles, too, seemed more tense and alert. What was it? What portent rode the night? What voice called out of the silence? The same forbidding obstacles remained, the same questions. And yet . . .

The twelve climbed to their lodgings in the upper room and spread their rugs about the floor. But none slept. A restless animation pervaded them, and they gave themselves over to prayer. "Oh Lord . . . cause thy face to shine upon us . . . that thy way may be known upon earth. . ." They prayed until dawn began silvering the walls of the upper room.

It was sunrise of Shabout, celebrating the moment when God blazed his law into the rock of Mt. Sinai, a time of thanksgiving, of inbringing of the first fruits, the 50th day after Passover—Pentecost! "And when the day of Pentecost was fully come . . ." Scripture recounts, "suddenly there came a sound from heaven as of a rushing mighty wind, and it filled all the house where they were sitting. And there appeared unto them, cloven tongues like as of fire, and it sat upon each of them. And they were all filled with the Holy Ghost . . ."

The time of waiting was over. The moratorium of the spirit had ended. They were ready now. They could go to work.

3.
Winds of the Morning

The hosts of humanity paused that day and pondered. It was an unlikely thing. Twelve shabby renegades shouting their exhortations in the streets. And the population heard. Men tried to turn away but their feet would not carry them. They sought to jeer but their throats filled. They contended but in vain. Preposterous! "The Day of the Spirit."

Joseph bar-Nabas, a wealthy, studious young Levite, could neither comprehend nor deny the surging response within him. His logic could find no grounds for the fact. It was Pentecost, the Jewish festival of the inbringing of first fruits, the eighth of Sivan, in the 15th year of the reign of Tiberius. Jerusalem swarmed with pilgrims of every nation and tongue.

And a crew of lawless rogues whose leader had been crucified seven weeks before cried their outrageous claims in the public thoroughfares, and hearts—by the hundreds—paused and pounded. Bar-Nabas beheld it, as in a daze.

At the "broad place" near the Damascus Gate, a throng massed around the lean-boned Galilean, John,

called Son of Thunder. He stabbed a finger at sky and
earth. "The Father has sent his son as the Savior of
the world!"

A myriad crowd pressed around, sheet-wrapped
Arabs, tall black Elamites, Phoenician sea captains,
imperial consuls, spiral-bearded Assyrians, Egyptians
in jeweled collars, shaven Greeks, Asians, men of every
shore. "He was in the world . . . the world knew him
not!" The voice spilled over them, a relentless tide.
"By this we know love, that he laid down his life for
us. . . . Love casts out fear. . . . He has given us of
his own Spirit!"

The formenters held forth on every hand—in the
crowded market plaza, under the porch of Bethesda
pool, on the pavement before the synagogue of the
Alexandrians, and in the teeming outer court of the
Temple. Bar-Nebas recognized most of them, having
seen them skulking about the house of his sister, Mary,
who in her sentimental widowhood had embraced the
cult. It had worried him. But now, with this uproar,
worse might befall. He wandered in the midst of it all,
appalled at it, yet also seized irrationally by it.

In the Temple quadrangle, the rough tones of the
fisherman, Peter beat like a drum roll. "God hath made
him both Lord and Christ, this Jesus whom you crucified." Hearers shoved closer, eyes wide, slack-jawed,
hands at their breasts, as he went on. "God raised him
up! We are all witnesses . . . the Holy Spirit he has
poured out!"

The incredibility of it could hardly have been greater.
A condemned cause! A "criminal's" progeny! The very
word, "crucified," was anathema in the mouths of
Israel. Yet this rabid nest had set the city agog. It
defied reason.

"They are drunk," a defensive shout arose at one
point. "They are filled with new wine!" Ah ha, that
was it, a little mockery should smash their spell. Yet
bar-Nabas knew it would not.

The man, Peter, dropped his arms and stood there, silent for a moment, and then resumed speaking, slowly, deliberately. "Give ear to my words. For these men are not drunk as you suppose, since it is only the third hour of the day." His point was obvious. Not even the morning meal came before the third hour, much less wine.

Something else, like bridled thunder, rode the morning air. Bar-Nabas, ever since rising at dawn from a fitful sleep, had felt the strange compulsion of it, like a humming in his ears. As he ventured into the streets, it intensified, even as he struggled against it.

Initially, he had no inkling of its cause. And then he had come first upon that firebrand John, atop some box or stone in the gateway square, his livid face flung back, extolling the slain Jesus. "In him was life, and life was the light of men! The light shines in the darkness." That weird vitality charged the air, gripped the listeners. "This is the victory that overcomes the world."

Bar-Nabas knew then the sense of his forebodings, that his sister and her son, John Mark, might be brought into jeopardy. For on this most volatile day of the year, the outcasts she harbored had loosed their wild foray. Surely the authorities would speedily strike it down. Yet simultaneously that other sensation caught hold of bar-Nabas and clung to him beyond his control. The voices of the expounders had an almost unearthly quality, ecstatic, boundless, as if borne on some invisible, animated current. It penetrated, not in the ordinary fashion of these men's common Aramaic speech, but by some peculiar multiloquence which seemed more vivid and intelligible than any familiar dialect. In bar-Nabas and around him the questions buzzed.

"Are not all these who are speaking Galileans? And how is it that we hear, each of us in his own native tongue?"

Whether only impression or objective reality, it had the same pervasive effect. It gripped each person in his own condition, an all-encompassing, universal speech like the Greek *Koine,* yet much more than that. Indeed, these rough Galileans spoke their native language, yet accompanied by an infinite clarity, a strength and transport which overcame divisions, as if one tongue had diffused into many, or many had combined into one.

"What does this mean?" the people exclaimed.

Bar-Nabas found himself remembering an ancient prophecy of Joel. ". . . I will pour out my spirit on all flesh . . . your old men shall dream dreams, and your young men shall see visions . . ."

With a start he realized that the man, Peter, was reciting that very augury, in his eerily expansive idiom. The thought, rather than the sound, had reached bar-Nabas, or both. He broke into a sweat, and the stabbing inflections went on, the strange magnetism of those voices.

"The day of the Lord! . . . The great and manifest day!"

A profound tension had fallen over the crowd, muffled, held in leash, like some stifled outcry. Finally it came, "What shall we do?" The sun blazed in bar-Nabas' eyes, and around him the stricken plea resounded, "What shall we do?"

"Repent and be baptized," Peter cried, "every one of you in the name of Jesus Christ for the forgiveness of sins . . ."

Bar-Nabas suspected in an instant's panic that they all, including himself, were succumbing to some gross sorcery, yet it surrounded him, a crushing demand, a pressure against his ribs, taking his breath, akin to death itself, and then at the bottom of his helplessness, he came into his own, into the clear, still place of knowing, of decision. A tenderness enfolded bar-Nabas;

he tasted the breath of spring and he dropped to his knees, conscious that many others had done likewise.

Three thousand were baptized that day. The fold of Christ, shrunken after the crucifixion to a tiny, fearful band of 120, suddenly had swelled into a fervent multitude. Thus the work commenced, not gradually, but with an abrupt, radical stroke.

Never had the impact of Jesus been so great. Crushed on the cross, his sway surged stronger than ever. No names are listed of the many converts that day, but subsequent records make clear that one of them, either that day, or shortly afterwards, was Joseph bar-Nabas, the scholarly young candidate for the Levitical priesthood. He sold his property, gave the proceeds to the poor and became a powerful, eloquent evangelist. He served as a co-missionary with Paul (after that impassioned toiler joined the cause), and worked later with his young kinsman, John Mark, extending the tidings from city to city.

That fresh wind that arose in Jerusalem carried men into paths which they had never expected to take.

4.
The Incorrigibles

An unexampled species, these Nazarenes. Gamaliel
eyed them perplexedly. They had brazenly flouted a
state edict. Yet for all his erudition, he could not come
to any clear judgment about them. Their conduct
mystified him. Their hymns, their "holy kisses," their
sharing of goods, the much-making over a common
gourd of wine, their constant smiles and indiscriminate
attachment for one another all seemed harmless
enough.

Yet their twelve leaders, arrested and arraigned before the council for the third time of late, were un-
questionably lawbreakers. And the dominant clique of
the Sanhedrin, in league with Rome, had decided in
advance that they must die. Gamaliel studied them dis-
passionately as they stood there before the railing,
guarded at either end. They were a roughcast, unedu-
cated lot, bronzed and coarsely mantled. They had a
bluff simplicity about them, doves for the snare. He
leaned back in his seat, his mouth set with sad cynicism
as the brusque preliminaries went forward.

A lofty-minded teacher, Gamaliel was master of the

famed school of Hillel, and the first of the great rabbis to be honored with the title, "rabban," an arch-scholar. But his status had waned in the Rome-dominated state-craft. He saw little hope for these culprits. Not that he held any brief for their bizarre "good news," equating God's awaited ruler with a crucified victim. But he preferred to let their claim fall of its own baselessness.

He sat in silence, his sagacious old eyes wearily disenchanted, as the summary hearing went on. Caiaphas, the high priest, fumed at the prisoners: "We strictly charged you not to teach in his name. Yet here you have filled Jerusalem with your teaching, and you intend to bring the man's blood upon us."

In the crackling revolutionary temper of the times, Rome had threatened stiff intervention at any failure of the Saducean collabroators in their oversight of religious affairs to keep down inflammatory movements. Yet the prisoners seemed unmoved by the gravity of their plight. These men not only were offenders, but prison-breakers. Twice before, since crucifixion of their Galilean inciter, they had been jailed and warned, "not to speak or teach at all in the name of Jesus." Once they had escaped, apparently through collusion of cell guards. And they persisted in their insubordination with unmitigated zeal.

They would not be let off lightly a third time. Lined up before the semicircular balustrade in the stone court chamber, the twelve exchanged stubborn looks and their ringleader, Peter, spoke in his mariner's growl: "We must obey God, rather than men."

It was sheer insolence. Gamaliel sighed resignedly as indignant exclamations broke out among the lawyers and ruling Sadducees. Caiaphas' face was purpled as lividly as his long embroidered meeir. "Marad! Rebellious!"

Opposing his Rome-upheld faction seemed useless. Yet Gamaliel, an inveterate old battler for principle, knew he must try. He counted several fellow Pharisees present who supported his doctrine of moderation, as against the severe school of Shamai. He had personally observed the conduct of the accused sect, noticing that its members continued in daily attendance at the Temple. They had not forsworn their ancestral faith, albeit they brought strange admixtures to it.

They had done no violence, despite tales of conspiratorial designs for a new kingdom. They were an abnormally affectionate folk, continually visiting one another, carrying gifts, breaking bread together, singing their songs, lifting those mystical flagons of wine.

Many were of the poor, the ebyonum, dwelling in the musty passages of the old eastern wall. Others were well off. But by their extraordinary charitableness, no Nazarene had an unfilled need. Yet they certainly had become a disturbance to the prevailing pattern of things. They created popular ferment, engendering reports of miraculous cures and supernatural intercessions. They attracted swarms of the afflicted.

Yet those who remained had increased until they now numbered 5,000 in Jerusalem alone, a small fragment in a city twenty times that, but nevertheless a sizeable force in these unstable times. Already, Rome's troops had stepped in repeatedly to stifle dissidence. Under this pressure, the Nazarenes had been banned as a conspiracy. And now the hothead, Peter, went on with his brash effrontry:

"The God of our Fathers raised up Jesus whom you killed by hanging him on a tree. God exalted him at his right hand as leader and Savior, to give repentance to Israel and forgiveness of sins. And we are witnesses to these things, and so is the Holy Spirit whom God has given to those who obey him."

At a signal from a Temple saghan, a guard slashed his whip across the fisherman's face, ordering silence. "Hosah! Hosah!" A paroxysm of rage seized the council. Gamaliel's pale hand tightened on his staff. The outburst reminded him of similar behavior by this very council before Rome executed the man of Nazareth. Gamaliel at that time had pleaded in vain for restraint. But he had failed. Now the memory of it crashed over him. He lunged to his feet, rapping his staff on the floor.

"Remove these men!" he commanded. "Return them to the dungeon! Let us reason calmly what must be done." Stunned attention fixed on the aging patriarch, and resentful murmurs surrounded him. But already the guards, stung by the imperious orders, herded the prisoners into a passage descending to the prison.

Gamaliel waited, his thoughts racing. Certainly he could not dispute the civil disobedience of these men. Nevertheless, as a liberal Pharisee, he also knew that God's loftiest concepts often sprang from ridiculed nonconformists. "Men of Israel," he said, "take care what you do with these men."

He hesitated, hemmed around by the glowering faces, by these power-jealous councilors straining to hang on to their shaky offices under the lash of Rome. Suddenly he saw their vulnerability. He knew how to beat them. They were afraid.

He nodded imperceptibly to himself. "These days," he went on, "the land trembles with contentions and alarms. The one titled our protector is even now called to account for scattering and slaying the Samaritan multitude on Mt. Gerizim. It is said the Eagle screams in Rome itself."

He paused, noting the uneasy reaction. The high priest squirmed, twisting his ring, as Gamaliel continued, suggesting the prudence of leaving the Nazarene sect to its own fate, like many others before it.

"Before these days, Theudas arose, giving himself out to be somebody," the rabbi went on. "A number of men, about 400 joined him, and he was slain and all who followed him were dispersed and came to nothing." Gamaliel cited other cases as well.

Then, amid the unsettled anxiety permeating the

chamber, he warned somberly, "So in the present case, I tell you, keep away from these men, and let them alone."

He saw the blanched, shaken reaction and heaped on a theological omen. "If this plan or this undertaking is of men, if will fail; but if it is of God, you will not be able to overthrow them. You might even be found opposing God!"

He sat down, eased of a burden. The court capitulated hastily, uncomfortably. For appearance's sake, it charged the group to speak no more "in the name of Jesus," had them flogged and let them go.

Gamaliel, the learned, idealistic Pharisee, a teacher of Saul or Tarsus, and possibly also of bar-Nabas, had raised a bold protest to save the apostles. And they went on teaching in the forbidden name of Jesus.

So did Saul, after a cereer of another kind.

5.
The Enforcer

The witnesses peeled off their tunics, passed them to Saul, and picked up large stones to heave at the man below. At the bottom of the rough hollow, Stephen stood looking up in dismay. An agitated crowd ringed the pit, smiting their chests, and shrieking denunciations. *"Blasphemeo! Anomos!"* Most of them were of Jerusalem's Greek-speaking Alexandrean and Cilician congregations. "Blasphemer! Transgressor!"

Saul, himself a Cilician, reared in the cosmopolitan city of Tarsus and a brilliant, forceful young rabbi, felt the blood pounding at his temples. The defiler had to be destroyed. He nodded. The first stones flew.

Under Roman rule, the occupation government could impose capital punishment in the form of stoning, burning, beheading, or strangling, subject in each case to confirmation by Rome's procurator. Stoning had been ordered for the nimble-tongued disrupter, Stephen, a functionary of the notorious brotherhood of *Christos*.

A corrupting menance, Saul adjudged. A gross offense against hallowed tradition and purity of faith. The land festered with wayward cults, and righteousness demanded that they be purged from the nation's sacred patrimony. That duty lay on him like a coat of nails, driving him to the utmost in devotion, dedication, and discipline. He would spare no effort to cleanse and preserve God's household. Yet he moaned as the barrage began on the condemned Stephen.

As required, the trial witnesses cast the first stones. Most of them missed the mark but one gashed the victim's shoulder and a heavy one thumped into his midriff, dropping him to his knees. "Behold," he cried out in the din,, "I see the heavens opened . . ."

The spectators, most of them stripped to their loin cloths, then joined in hurling the stones which thudded and clattered about him, lacerating his flesh. One whirring missile smashed an eye into a bloody pulp. Saul twisted and untwisted the garments in his hands, the migraine gathering at the front of his skull.

Three years or more had gone by since the man of Nazareth was crucified, a strictly Roman punishment, and the feverish impressions about him had continued to spread.

To Saul, it was a poisonous malady, eroding the vitals of Judaism, a macabre contradiction about a common Galilean who died shamefully, obviously abandoned by God, yet elevated in his ignominy to Messianic status. The infection had been scattered by travelers to many surrounding cities, where cells multiplied, and in Jerusalem itself, it had spilled beyond Aramaic and Hebrew speaking groups to Greek-language synagogues.

In one of these, the eloquent and literate Stephen had aroused antagonism by his claim that a "Holy Spirit" loosed by the *Christos* now transcended nation and rite. He struck at the very ramparts of the nation's sacred heritage. Accusers told authorities that he spoke ceaselessly "against this holy place and the law." A crowd, accompanied by officials, hunted him out and dragged him before the court.

Only a few weeks earlier, Stephen had been appointed by the apostles as one of seven assistants, or deacons, to oversee the distribution of goods to the needy among their numbers. Now, he faced a quick end to his short-lived assignment.

He made a lengthy defense before the court, recounting God's work throughout the length of Jewish history, crowned by the work of Jesus. But the accusers prodded him and he ended with a damning burst of excoriation, even at the Temple itself. "The Most High does not dwell in houses made with hands," he declared. "You stiff-necked people, uncircumcised in heart and ears, you always resist the Holy Spirit . . . Which of the prophets did your fathers persecute? And . . . the Righteous One . . . you have now betrayed and murdered."

Condemned, he was hustled out of the city to the stoning pit. And Saul, whose name in its Roman version was Paul, stood by as a deputy for the court to see the execution carried out.

Scripture recounts: "Saul laid waste the church, and entering house after house, he dragged off men and women and committed them to prison." Yet all the while, anxiety and compassion raked his conscience.

He pitied even as he punished. He shuddered at the obstinancy of these Jesus believers. His great teacher, Gamaliel, disapproved. He could no longer sleep.

The persecution had dispersed many heretics to outlying regions. He, too, would go elsewhere. He would get away. But he would not give up. The Book of Acts relates: "Saul, still breathing threats and murder against the disciples of the Lord, went to the high priest and asked him for letters to the synagogues at Damascus" to arrest deviants and bring them bound to Jerusalem for trial.

While on his way there, in the vortex of his desolating struggle, he had his staggering vision of Christ. "Saul, Saul, why do you persecute me?" And Saul gave in. The thundering enforcer surrendered; the ruler for God became the ruled. He lay flat on his face, a broken man, and so made whole.

"It is no longer I who live," he later wrote, "but Christ who lives in me." In a kind of death, he came alive. Shorn of self, he found a great self. "If any one is in Christ, he is a new creation." So the strange phenomenon, the night through which breaks the day, the fall which becomes the rising. And Saul, Paul, by whatever name, mounted the long and arduous road lit through the shadows of a cross.

Not that he foreswore his ancestral faith, quite the contrary, cherished it fervently, a Hebrew, a son of Abraham. "I am a Pharisee, the son of a Pharisee," he declared. But he also was the foremost missionary and advocate of the greatest Hebrew of all, Jesus of Nazareth. Paul roamed the first-century world disseminating faith in him and the gift of his life to mankind.

It cost Paul dearly. Five times, he recounted, he was lashed, three times beaten with rods, once stoned, three times shipwrecked, endangered by robbers, by his own people, by Gentiles, by wilderness, hunger, cold, exposure and hardship.

But he worked on. So did the others. And they, too,

paid. The apostle James was executed in Jerusalem by Herod Agrippa. The other apostles were dispersed, stubbornly teaching, encouraging, dying.

The days were fierce. Less than three decades after Christ's crucifixion, revolution engulfed Judea to be crushed by Rome in vast slaughter and destriction which ended Jewish nationhood for 1,882 years until 1948. In that ancient period of turbulance, thousands of Christians and Jews were slain for their faith in Palestine, Egypt, Rome and elsewhere. In Rome, tradition says, Peter was crucified and Paul beheaded. And that harsh suppression would go on, in many times and places, from Nero's circus to Red Square, Belsen and Indo-China, from Angola to South Africa to the ghettos of America, the crosses and the flame, the dying for life.

It was the kind of fate which Paul had once helped visit on another, Stephen, the outspoken deacon in Jerusalem, the first of the long line of Christian martyrs.

As the stones had rained on him, and his bloodied torn body crumpled toward the ground, his shattered face turned upward and his voice throbbed with awareness of a further door opening before him. "Lord Jesus, receive my spirit."

Then he cried out loudly, "Lord, do not hold this sin against them!" And he died in the heap of stones. Paul could never forget it; the image stayed with him until the blade fell on his own neck.

And also the cry, the cry which started at another execution, the cry which Jesus gave from the cross, and which ignited a fire of forgiveness and regeneration to shine even after through the crucifixions of the world:

"Father, forgive them, for they know not what they do."

d cannon ... closing the undeserved devotion of